REDEFINING THE POWER OF MENTORING

HOW CAN YOU SERVE AS A ROLE MODEL FOR OTHERS BY EXHIBITING YOUR UNIQUE QUALITIES, TRAITS, AND BEHAVIOURS THAT THE PERSON YOU'RE MENTORING CAN EMULATE?

DR. AMIT DAS

To

All my bosses and mentors who made a difference in my professional career.

"It would be hard to list all the ways you have helped my professional development. I genuinely appreciate all that you have done for me, and I can only hope that one day I will be able to repay the favour. Not only have you been a great mentor to me, but you have also inspired me to become a great mentor to others. I appreciate you setting a strong example. I appreciate you being such an example and a visionary mentor. I am really grateful for and treasure what you have taught me. I'm grateful."

- Dr. Amit Das, Motivational Speaker, Leadership Coach and Mentor.

Contents

Foreword

Dear Reader,

This book covers all aspects of successful mentoring, including how to become a mentor, how to engage mentees, and how to encourage individuals to realise their maximum potential. This book teaches how to locate a good fit when pairing mentors and mentees, how to foster a supportive atmosphere, and how to assess improvement.

It provides a general review of the ideal mentoring techniques and issues a call to action for capable leaders to take on the role of mentor. This book gives a road map for developing the finest in budding professionals and demonstrates how the act may enable employees to become their best selves. This book examines mentoring from the standpoints of both the mentor and the mentee.

> *"One of the most beneficial books for workplace mentorship is this one."*

It gives multiple useful tips to help you learn the subtleties that underpin purposeful growth and is packed with real-world examples. By reading this book, you can become the greatest mentor you can be, provide your mentees with unique experiences, and leave a lasting legacy.

This book teaches readers how to intentionally and successfully mentor others. It is a simple, direct guide for assisting mentors in all institutions, organisations, and enterprises to become outstanding mentors to others. The author draws on years of experience as a specialist in mentoring relationships and workplace mentoring problems, as well as considerable research.

"Excellence is facilitated by a willingness to learn."

There are countless disciplines from which we might select to sample and then apply the teachings to our daily lives. Here, the author described many examples in which senior management executives had seized the chance to educate the younger executives they had been mentoring on business matters.

> *"Being interested keeps the mind open to new ideas, and learning is a mindset that knows no age limits."*

The book discusses the many stages of mentoring and looks at how the relationship might change as it goes along. This book demonstrates for both parties how to establish clear goals and expectations, encourage and test one another, provide and accept feedback, and create new targets as the trip progresses.

This book highlights that mentoring is a two-way process and a team-learning activity, and demonstrates how the relationship may be advantageous to both sides.

The resource you'll refer to time and time again is methods of successful mentoring, regardless of whether mentoring is a calling or a choice, if you're new to it or an experienced pro, if you're in a structured programme or on your own.

In addition to managing your team members, it is your job as a leader to guide them toward realising their full potential and achieving success on a personal level. For those who want to help others realise their full potential and accomplish their career goals, such as leaders, coaches, mentors, and consultants, this book is the ideal resource.

This is one of the more beneficial books about mentorship programmes. This book offers a planning framework for creating mentoring programmes that endure and provide outcomes. The book describes the traits of successful programmes and offers advice to leaders on how to design interactions that benefit all parties involved. This book offers a how-to for businesses aiming to develop future leaders and delivers a systematic approach to mentoring.

While most mentoring materials focus on the mentee or the programme, this book is specifically designed to assist you in being a successful mentor. In this book, the author offers advice on how to develop your mentoring skills to provide significant benefits for both you and your mentee. Dr. Amit Das explores tried-and-true methods to apply in your continuing sessions, such as enhancing the power of questions, utilising experience for learning, and fostering growth using common psychology, drawing on more than 12 years of experience working with mentors.

This Book about powerful mentoring are nonfiction publications that outline the optimal procedure for professional growth. This book offers suggestions on how to create and take part in successful mentoring programmes for mentors, mentees, and organisations. This book includes subjects including pairing mentors and mentees, providing feedback, making goals for professional growth, and evaluating the outcomes of mentoring initiatives.

The author offers clear guidelines for becoming a helpful mentor. The book begins by outlining and describing the mentor relationship before sharing guidelines, best practises, qualities of effective mentors, and typical hazards.

The author offers specific guidance on how to inspire and assist mentees, direct their development, and get beyond obstacles that can impede or halt progress. The content is broken up with tools like reflection questions, checklists, exercises, and tips and suggestions in the book's textbook-like, readily scannable style. This book may assist mentors in structuring the process so that both sides obtain wonderful outcomes in exchange for the time and effort they put in.

The relationship between mentor and mentee is what makes mentoring genuinely transformational and more than just an organisational duty. But building in a virtual environment is also quite difficult. The author's definition of rapport includes robust communication, common values and viewpoints, mutual trust and respect. Particularly for individuals who are underrepresented in your organisation or sector, the calibre of this personal connection is essential for keeping personnel.

His examples include checklists for setting up a mentoring relationship; discussion points for meetings; sample agendas; instructions for tasks; and questions to put to mentees in a range of situations. The book explains proper mentorship protocol and instructs mentors on how to plan fruitful sessions and assess mentees' development over the course of the programme.

"Mentorship is much more than just dispensing sporadic advice."

This book may also assist mentees in selecting a mentor and managing their own personal growth, which is particularly helpful if an organisation does not already have robust mentoring programmes in place.

The author of this book lays out a thorough, step-by-step strategy for mentoring, developing, and coaching others. Dr. Amit Das speaks eloquently and passionately about something that many leaders overlook: that being a leader is all about helping people grow. The technique for assisting people in becoming the best versions of themselves by finding job success and personal contentment will be specifically and thoroughly described in the book.

Additionally, it will encourage readers to remember their most outstanding instructors or guide, enjoy the richness of their own life experiences, and keep pursuing chances to become mentors that matter the most for themselves.

Get your copy today to get started on your mentoring journey!

So, happy reading and learning to all my readers.

Carpe diem.

Dr. Amit Das

Motivational Speaker, Leadership Coach, and Mentor.

Preface

"Enlarge people's horizons; maintain momentum for growth; promote substantial professional progress. To complete all of this, no workplace superhero is required. You can accomplish it after you develop into a skilled mentor."

Businesses are now changing quickly, so in five to ten years, your industry may appear quite different. Your capacity to adapt, your openness to learning, and your desire to work with others will be key factors in your ability to progress and acquire the abilities you need to prosper.

"Mentorships are excellent vehicles for this sort of development, especially when both sides gain from the connection."

As we struggled to deal with the global effects of a pandemic, our emotional and mental health were put to the test. These difficulties might show up as exhaustion or a lack of ability to make judgments. You might be able to handle certain emotional issues at work with the aid of a mentor. Your transition to the computer business might be hampered by microaggressions, impostor syndrome, and other feelings of inadequacy.

"A mentor can assist you in identifying the precise ways you contribute to teams and add value to your organisation."

Mentors have been one of the most significant people in your career or personal life, so it is imperative to express your gratitude. Any business may benefit from mentor resources' assistance in using technology to establish specialised, low-cost career development programmes. Due to my experience as both a mentor and a mentee, I am writing this book.

I have rarely mentored more than two students at once. Although I could coach a small group of four people, I don't suggest using this strategy. I advise taking on no more than two mentees for the best experience. When I once took on a third mentee, it was at the request of one of my old colleague, who wanted to give the employee more opportunities to learn. Nobody benefits when you or your mentees are overextended.

> *"If done properly, mentoring can be a valuable—and effective—way to engage and retain talent. It can be a gratifying experience for both mentors and mentees. Additionally, you're fostering long-term development for yourself as you help others have more fulfilling work experiences."*

During my most recent mentoring experience, my mentees and I created a presentation and a resource list about how to make accessible films. Everyone needs to enjoy themselves. You'll note that a lot of my views apply to both mentors and mentees. This is mostly because, although while I serve as a mentor and offer advice, the relationship is two-way; I learn just as much from the people I mentor. The mentees' inquiries about what I have done, what I do, or how I do it drive me to view things from a new angle, and I take advantage of their curiosity to find new approaches to problems. There's that win-win scenario we discussed. These ideas are not exhaustive, so I'd love to hear your opinions.

I've discovered that the best mentoring enables a mentee to choose a certain path to take and develops the abilities required to do so. A mentor can help you decide whether or not that particular qualification makes sense for your professional path and point you in the direction of alternatives. I really believe that taking concrete actions will help you determine your success.

You have been a fantastic leader who has selflessly devoted a substantial amount of his life to assisting young people who choose the proper route to pursue.

- How is excellence defined and demonstrated?
- What separates coaching from counselling and mentorship?
- How can a good mentor strike a balance between facts and larger perspective, words and deeds, to help bring about change?
- How can we best remember our teachers and share the blessings they gave us?
- What can we learn from the inspirational people we have met about how to become mentors, role models, and mentors ourselves?
- What abilities do you acquire via mentoring?
- What are those benefits of mentoring relationships for both mentor and mentee?
- What is the significance of workplace mentoring programmes and the reasons for their widespread use?
- How to launch a mentoring programme?
- How to initiate mentorship programme in remote or hybrid organisations?

I became a mentor because I wanted to support someone and improve their career and life. Mentoring a student from a different management school helped the mentee and I do discuss any problems more openly, since I could act as an impartial sounding board without knowing the individuals involved. Although I make an effort to adhere to certain guidelines, each mentoring session has evolved to suit the requirements of the mentee.

The ideal strategy wasn't necessarily my forthright manner. I would thus ask my mentor to review my points and offer suggestions before delivering comments. I eventually mastered the ability to provide feedback that is more attentive, precise, and sympathetic.

I hope that my mentees have benefited from our regular meetings, which have given them the chance to practise difficult conversations, choose their course of action, and be held accountable, as well as from simply having a private place to voice their worries in a comfortable, judgment-free environment.

The book discusses issues including developing relationships with others, networking, and cooperating. The book's provides information on how to become a mentor, how to start a mentorship programme inside of a company, and how to tell coaching from mentoring. A continuing narrative that follows the development of a main fictional character through a mentoring relationship serves as the book's main plot device and exemplifies these concepts. It presents a quick crash course in mentoring to participants on both sides of the equation.

Mentorship has been a crucial component of my professional development. Focus on communicating and listening, offering helpful constructive feedback, and developing empathy if you're in the mentoring position and want to improve.

Did you know that one of Mark Zuckerberg's mentors, Steve Jobs, contributed to the success of Facebook as the most widely used social network worldwide?

Did you set any career-related resolutions for the new year?

Are you determined to advance professionally and advance your career in 2023?

If so, you might think about mentoring, a little-used yet very effective professional development technique. So now is the ideal opportunity to learn more about the advantages of mentoring for your career. The mentoring connection, whether you are the mentor or the mentee, may advance your career to new heights.

When should coaching be used instead of mentoring, counselling, or coaching?

I'll teach you what to look for, how to locate one, and how to create a successful connection that benefits you both if you're thinking about hiring a mentor to assist with your ongoing work obligations and long-term career ambitions.

> *"The integrity of the mentor position may be compromised if the organisation has a predetermined objective for the mentoring relationship that neither the mentor nor the mentee are involved in."*

This book will examine the parallels, discrepancies, and appropriate times for each. It is a book for mentoring people who come from very various origins, identities, and viewpoints. For instance, mentees from different generations or mentees of various ethnicities or cultures.

This book demonstrates how to challenge mentees while remaining cognizant of and respectful of such differences.

Not all mentors have more life experience or maturity than you have. My mentor is a younger person than I am, but he or she has a lot more years of expertise in a certain field.

The success of both you and your mentee can be improved by mentoring. Make 2023 the year you make a significant investment in mentoring, and you'll see the benefits throughout your career. One of the best things you can do for your job and personal growth is to engage in a mentorship relationship, which is frequently mentioned.

I will teach you how to strike up a connection, find common ground, and promote development in these various mentoring situations. In contrast to pushing mentees into a mould, the book teaches mentors how to comprehend and sympathise with their mentees and assists mentees in becoming the greatest versions of themselves. All chapters in this book include subjects including admitting privilege and bias, getting to know one another, and giving constructive criticism. In a time when workforces are expanding at an ever-increasing rate, the book bridging differences for better mentoring is particularly crucial.

"You have done a great job as a leader, a supervisor, a teacher, and most of all, a friend. You possess every trait a mentor seeks in a mentee, and I will always be appreciative of that. Working with you has been a very unforgettable experience, and you have prepared me to be a competent professional. I will always be grateful for your help and generosity."
-Dr. Amit Das

PREFACE

Acknowledgements

At the outset, I will thank my family for supporting me throughout the journey of writing my book and encouraging me to live my dreams; my son has always been instrumental in giving his inspiration to complete the writing of this book. Despite the fact that I am listed as the author of this book, "Redefining The Power Of Mentoring" would not have been published if I had depended entirely on my own talents. Creating this book required more than anything—it took a family of dedicated and caring people who were always prepared to lend a hand.

Writing a book while working full-time is no simple task, so I'd want to express my gratitude to my amazing coworkers who act as cheerleaders in equal measure. Thank you, too, to my students and clients for your patience and unflinching support while I worked on this book!

Thank you to everyone who has listened to me argue for doing everything you can to make your life, including your work life, more progressive. I appreciate everyone's assistance throughout the process. This book would not have been possible without each of you having had an impact on my life in some manner.

Lastly, I would like to thank all the people with whom I have been associated. You gave me power. I would like to thank Notion Press for publishing my book. Finally, thank you all for gifting your time to read this book.

I'd want to convey my heartfelt appreciation to the almighty God for bestowing his blessings and being so gracious.

Redefining Mentorship And It's Framework

"The delicate balance of mentoring someone is not creating them in your own image, but giving them the opportunity to create themselves." — Steven Spielberg

A mentor speeds up our progress by illuminating a path for us that is less complicated and fraught with difficulties.

The word "mentor" originally appeared in ancient Greek literature, in Homer's epic "The Odyssey," in which Odysseus spent 20 years away from home battling and wandering. During that period, Telemachus, the son he had abandoned as a baby, grew up under the watchful eye of Mentor, an old trusted friend. When the goddess Athena decided it was time to finish young Telemachus' education, she came to him disguised as Mentor, and the two of them set off to learn about his father. Since then, the character's name has become a slang phrase for "trustworthy tutor." Mentors have existed since people first walked the world. If we didn't have mentors, we would have to learn everything from scratch every time we started a new activity.

"A mentor may provide a mentee with a wide range of benefits. Mentors have a variety of skills, such as: listening, imparting wisdom, posing probing questions."

Mentorship has evolved into a collaborative process of mutual discovery where both the mentor and mentee have contributions to make to the relationship (the "give") and contributions to make that will extend their own views (the "get").

"Being a mentee may make you feel as though you have to be transparent about all your difficulties and failings. In any case, mentoring may be scary. It need not, however, feel that way."

According to Wikipedia, a mentor is someone who instructs or offers assistance and advice to a less experienced and frequently younger individual. A mentor has an impact on a mentee's personal and professional development in an organisational environment. It is important that mentors have experience from which others might learn.

"Mentoring as a connection between two people in which one person with more rank, experience, or competence teaches, directs, or assists others to improve both professionally and personally."

Since a mentoring relationship that develops naturally rather than being required as a deliverable by the organisation offers greater value, it is better for all parties involved.

A mentor is a seasoned individual who served as a trusted advisor as the professional navigated the path up the corporate ladder. If you ask any thoroughbred professional to list the top three critical factors in their achievements, there is a very high likelihood that they will include a mentor among them.

It's priceless to have someone who can extract years of hard-won knowledge in a week or two. We now use the term "mentor" to denote someone who has a constructive, guiding influence on another's life.

"A formalised collaboration between coworkers to promote learning and progress in a business or academic institution is known as mentoring."

The sharing and development of knowledge is a key objective of mentoring, and mentors must seek to promote both situational and thematic learning in pertinent professional fields. Such specialised mentorship aids in reducing the learning curve and increasing worker productivity.

Is mentoring still possible today?

Although I believe it is still possible to find a mentor, empathy and compassion are now more crucial than ever. It's crucial for you to understand as a mentee that your potential mentor can be overburdened with work and family commitments. Stay flexible in your relationship; this can include communicating largely via email or adjusting how often you meet.

The mentor possesses the skills and information necessary to pass them on to the mentee. He is a skilled active listener who is skilled at providing constructive criticism beneficial to the mentee's job progress.

"A mentor is a skilled expert who has a wealth of experience and information to impart to a mentee. A mentor is someone who acts as a role model, advisor, and motivator while also exuding adoration and respect."

People are frequently split into two categories: mentors and mentees. But it only makes sense in a society that is relatively stable, where the structures and lessons of the past are still relevant today. Today, innovative approaches are at least as useful as time-tested ones, and everyone can help us find solutions to the world's biggest and most pressing issues.

A mentor that has the potential to actually transform is built on this spark. Don't put yourself in a box. As a result, mentoring is no longer a one-way path; as a mentee, you can mentor others in the same ways that you may educate and influence your mentor. You may share the knowledge you have received through your own mentoring and reflect on your strengths and weaknesses by doing this.

"At its foundation, mentoring is about giving individuals the chance to learn from one another. It makes it possible for information to be shared between two or more individuals for the good of everyone."

People can share knowledge and learn from one another through mentorship. An experienced professional could mentor a less experienced coworker in the workplace by sharing knowledge and concepts. While students in academic institutions can discuss educational and job prospects with a mentor, recent graduates can learn how to plan out a professional route and make contacts for future employment.

"At a critical juncture, they all open their lives to us. And they all look at the same basic issues."

Anyone who has been a transformative instructor may also refer to themselves as mentors at times. More frequently, it's someone who plays a different position in our lives, such as a parent, pastor, kid, manager, friend, therapist, role model, or hero. Anyone interested in personal development, education in all of its forms, or the progression of successful lives will turn to a mentor.

Why do we need someone to assist us in improving our lives?

Mentorship at work can encourage employees to learn and improve by exposing them to new learning opportunities and providing assistance. Mentor-mentee relationships are frequently mutually developmental for both mentor and mentee. In the Ramayana, we learn about Hanuman, who was inspired to fly across the sea by Jambavant. In the Mahabharata, Krishna was Arjuna's instructor. Many figures in Indian history were trained by their mentors, such as Chandragupta Maurya by Kautilya, Swami Vivekananda by Ramakrishna Paramahamsa, and Pandit Nehru by Mahatma Gandhi, to name a few. Mentorship was used to pass down ancient knowledge and talents from one generation to the next.

Both the mentee and the mentor profit from effective mentoring. The most obvious advantage for a mentee is access, typically to the mentor's knowledge or counsel. Because a mentor's benefits are largely intangible, it can be difficult to see their value at times. Either way, mentoring is advantageous for the mentor in some manner, whether it is because it makes them feel good or because they were mentored and want to pay it forward.

> *"A mentor is someone who gives you advice on how to develop your abilities, make wiser choices, and obtain fresh perspectives on your life and profession. Your mentor will use their experience to help you now and in the future with your professional or personal life as a mentee. A mentor is someone you may go to for guidance and a role model to emulate rather than learning by doing."*

Selecting a mentor is the first and most crucial step. Be aware that you will have a variety of mentors throughout your career depending on the stages or pathways you choose, and just as the mentors will change, so will your connections with them.

How and when to employ mentoring, counselling, and coaching?

Each of the three approaches—coaching, counselling, and mentoring—has its advantages and appropriate times to use them. There are several areas where coaching, counselling, and mentoring are similar. There are significant distinctions, though. They are all really versatile and potent human relationships that can help you advance both personally and professionally. Depending on the internal and external problems that an individual experiences, each of these connections may play a significant role in a person's professional and life path. They can even be more effective when utilised in tandem to accelerate progress and outcomes.

While comparable, the main distinction between a coach and a consultant is that a consultant shares their experience to assist you in achieving a specific objective. According to the conventional perspective, consultants are frequently hired specifically to provide advice based on predetermined areas of competence. Your coach will help you discover your own solutions for overcoming obstacles and achieving your objectives. When hiring a coach, you want someone who has experience dealing with people just like you.

Coaching books educate leaders how to give broad advice, but mentoring books offer readers how to draw on their own personal expertise and experience to support mentees in realising their full potential. While mentoring involves a more regimented method, coaching is typically a more relaxed procedure. Additionally, coaching may be carried out in a group setting, whereas mentoring calls for a one-on-one one.

What distinguishes mentoring from coaching and counselling, and how do they compare?

Some of the important distinctions are outlined in the following table. Some people may make use of consulting services in addition to coaching, counselling, and mentoring. Let's start with basic definitions before we discuss the differences between coaching, counselling, and mentoring.

While coaching, counselling, and mentoring have certain similarities, each also has very clear differences and advantages. They are all helpful for certain situations, objectives, and requirements; none of them are inherently superior to the others. In fact, some people will engage in all three at once because they feel that each is profitable in its own way.

"Mentoring is a relationship between two individuals in which the one with greater experience, knowledge, and connections is able to pass on what they have learned to a more junior individual within a certain sector."

As is clear from the definitions, although the subject matter of these partnerships and dialogues differ, all three require interpersonal relationships.

"Counseling involves helping people with physical, emotional, and mental health concerns enhance their sense of well-being, lessen feelings of distress, and resolve crises."

It's simple to provide counsel. However, the ability to determine whether or not the advice you offer will be helpful to the recipient is a talent.

"Coaching is described as partnering with clients in a thought-provoking and creative process that motivates them to fulfil their personal and professional potential."

Additionally, each differs along a continuum from more prescriptive, directive telling and advice-giving on the one hand, to more open facilitation of introspection and contemplation on the other. Each connection also serves a unique purpose and will generally be more acceptable and helpful in some circumstances than others.

Does someone have to be in our lives for a very long time to have an influence on us?

I think back on my mentor. He was one of the first individuals to tell me that I didn't have to apologise for desiring a sense of balance in my life. We've been in touch, and he continues to assist me in calibrating and prioritising some important aspects of my life. He showed me how to break down the problems at hand, build effective slides, and present ideas to clients. What I really appreciated was how he did it in such an objective way. He placed my excitement and needs above his interests.

> *"Our mentors are the ones that light the fire in our hearts when it comes to business. We all need mentors. They motivate us, assist us in difficult situations, and direct our paths."*

What would your organisation's scorecard look like if you scored yourselves as employers who empower your people holistically to be more effective in their jobs?

You will agree that, by any measure, the corporate climate is unpredictable. Isn't it?

Internal and external dynamics play a role in the constantly shifting path that enterprises must take on a daily basis. Are we asking ourselves this as people leaders before sketching up development programmes and mapping them to organisational needs? Some of the more forward-thinking ones devised a "mentor-mentee" programme for mid-level managers that extends beyond the original hiring process and serves as a formative role for them, with the goal of strengthening their competencies and preparing them for more senior responsibilities.

By utilising technology, you can make the most of accessible mentorship relationships. When looking at mentor-mentee relationships, it's important to remember that the mentor-mentee connection is a two-way street. By looking beyond your organisation and engaging with your professional network, you may cast a broad net for mentorship possibilities.

> *"A mentoring culture allows organisation to bring on board not only profitable but also fascinating ideas, boosting their innovation quotient and giving them a competitive advantage."*

This, in my opinion, is the one that provides the most bang for the buck, given that it is not something that the organisation has mandated as a deliverable and is based on a relationship. You may be aware that many of the most well-known businesspeople in the world have mentors. They recognise that success is not a one-person show, and that mentors can assist them in keeping their company current and inventive. With so many of the world's most notable executives going on record to thank a mentor for part of their success, the relationship between a mentor and a mentee can be the most influential in business.

> *"Mentorship is one of the most underappreciated and underutilised talent management techniques."*

Mentorship has the potential to help individuals for a lifetime. If you're in charge of a team in today's workplace, you're probably dealing with numerous generations—often up to four! As the workplace experiences a significant demographic shift, multigenerational management has become a hot issue in recent months. Despite the fact that different generations have had diverse life experiences, we all have more in common than we know. Most of us would benefit from having a mentor who could assist us at work and serve as a guide and sounding board as we progress in our careers.

According to Forbes, mentorship programmes are offered by 84% of Fortune 500 organisations. Contrarily, according to another survey, 94% of workers stated they would remain at a business longer if given the chance to advance their careers. More than 90% of small companies acknowledge that mentoring helps them expand, advance, and accomplish their objectives.

> *"Mentorship is a natural action in which we all participate without even realising it. Whether you want to be mentored to acquire a new skill, advance in your careers, or gain a new perspective, you all want to improve yourselves."*

Mentorship teaches mentors a lot about themselves, and they can use what they've learned to tackle their own difficulties and challenges in new and better ways. Which is why mentorship has been regarded as a crucial part in the success of many of the world's most renowned people, including Bill Gates and Bill Clinton. Traditional mentoring methods have failed to keep up with advances in today's corporate environment, despite the clear benefits of mentoring. As a result, promote and sustain mentoring at your company by emphasising its importance and stressing how connections serve as a catalyst for transformation for both mentors and mentees. Also, create formal mentorship programmes that allow workers to participate in personal and professional growth that is directed by the organisation's structure.

"For someone who is going through that experience for the first time, hearing how someone else addressed an issue is always instructive."

Let's be open to forming a mentorship connection with someone who is different from us in terms of race, gender, or age—it can help us get new ideas and views on others' work experiences.

What to look for in a mentor and why?

Finding someone who possesses the ideal balance of mentorship qualities is not an easy feat. Although many people possess the qualities necessary to make effective mentors, they lack the time. An effective mentor-mentee relationship requires work on both sides. It won't work without commitment.

"Mentorship is a two-way relationship, just like any other. To increase their network of contacts in the business world, mentors seek mentees with robust networks. So invest time in expanding your network and cultivating your contacts. You never know who may be a potential mentor for someone."

- A good mentor should be prepared to pick up the phone, write a kind email, or arrange to meet for coffee. If not, the partnerships may end abruptly. Of course, the mentee has a lot of work to do to maintain the ties. But in return for the mentee's efforts, the mentor must be able to provide assistance.
- Everybody has certain advantages and disadvantages. A competent mentor is aware of this and makes an effort to find out what makes their mentee tick.

Even if you already know your advantages and disadvantages, it might be useful to get a second opinion. For instance, I think of myself as a good communicator. But one of my mentors suggested a few years ago that I add more empathy to my remarks.

- An excellent mentor is both motivating and approachable. They have the time to listen and a thriving profession of their own. They offer candid criticism and are sympathetic.
- When seeking a mentor, people sometimes feel overwhelmed since there are so many factors to take into account. The fact is, not every mentor has an equal influence. Some may have been extraordinary, while others may have been more focused on their egos and concerns.

Building a successful career requires finding a suitable mentor. Mentors may help you develop the skills you need to advance your career, offer advice on how to handle difficult coworkers, and expose you to their wide network. The advantages are innumerable. You must now identify someone who is suitable. You can even attempt to train to become your own mentor. In any case, we'll go through what a mentor is and what characteristics to watch for so you can spot an excellent mentor when they cross your path.

- A mentor supports their mentee in being held responsible for their aims. The mentor keeps the mentee motivated and on track to fulfil them by monitoring progress.

- Additionally, it may make sure that the mentee does not lose sight of their objectives. Knowing that someone is watching might help motivate a mentee since they don't want to disappoint their mentor by falling short of their objectives.
- A mentor can assist their mentee in developing personal or professional objectives. They can formulate SMART goals—specific, attainable, relevant, and time-based—for efficient goal-setting. These These objectives might help the mentee concentrate their efforts and make it simpler for the mentor to monitor and evaluate progress. When pursuing a bigger goal, they could break it down into smaller activities in order to achieve certain goals or acquire certain abilities.
- Mentors who can pay attention and think about the material they are provided frequently have a better understanding of you as a person. Their recommendations are more pertinent to you because they are aware of your unique background and position.

One of my mentors frequently listens to me go about problems without giving any guidance. Instead, they elicit information from me so that I may draw my own judgments. My ability to solve problems and make decisions with confidence have both improved as a result.

> *"Mentoring involves having the ability to communicate stories that contain personal experiences, case studies, and honest insight. It also entails actively listening; asking compelling, open-ended questions; reflecting on oneself; offering criticism; and being able to share stories."*

Having said that, there is no set period of time required for effective mentoring. It depends on who is involved and how the connection is structured. A mentor and you may have a conversation once every three months or have lunch once a month.

- A good mentor should be more than just a prosperous person. An effective mentor must have the mindset and desire to help others grow. It necessitates a readiness to consider and communicate one's own experiences, even failures. In addition to talking the talk, great mentors must also "walk the walk."
- An excellent mentor is really interested in assisting another person without expecting any "formal" compensation. Genuinely wanting to see someone else succeed is the motivation behind good mentors' actions. Mentors need to share both their "how I did it right" and their "how I did it wrong" tales. Both events provide priceless chances to learn.

Willingness and ability to devote genuine time and effort to the mentoring relationshipIt takes time to be a mentor; good intentions are insufficient. current and pertinent knowledge, skills, and/or experience related to the industry or organisation.

> *"The finest mentors are experts in the field that their mentee aspires to pursue."*

- The most experienced and effective mentors are aware that the foundation of their finest work as a mentor is not built on their knowledge and years of problem-solving. It is considerably more important how they interact with their mentee, so mentors must learn and use certain growth-promoting strategies.

- A corporate mentor should have the following abilities like clearly defining the findings, a desire to share their expertise and abilities; skills in synthesis and listening; assertiveness and sympathy; has the capacity to encourage learning; understanding how to use the question as a tool for introspection and establishing a trustworthy environment and connection; passion for helping others; possibility of providing continuing feedback and ability to challenge and expose new views personal and professional dedication to assisting the mentee.

- Excellent mentors are aware of the value of purposeful instruction and active listening. Before making recommendations, they inquire into the problem from all possible angles. Sometimes they do nothing except listen.

> *"People are the lifeblood of your company, and enlisting them in your transformational journey demands a clear vision that yields workable solutions. This is only achievable if employees are aware of the organisation's objective and vision, as well as how important their job is to the overall picture."*

- Honest comments may be given in a mentoring relationship built on trust. Building trust teaches the mentee that constructive criticism is designed to help them improve professionally rather than to be hurtful. By pointing out opportunities for growth, mentors may assist mentees. Since this is a business connection, the mentor has an impartial function to perform. A buddy could be reluctant to point out the mentee's shortcomings because they don't want to come across as judgmental.

- Mentors must be trustworthy since you could disclose to them things that you wouldn't otherwise divulge. Any mentor-mentee relationship must be able to handle uncomfortable talk if it is to succeed and benefit both parties.
- The relationship between a mentor and a mentee is comparable. It is a collaboration, and like any partnership, it has the potential to be very beneficial for both parties. It offers the chance for both parties to get exposure to many points of view, improve their communication abilities, and consider novel approaches to problem-solving.
- Trust is a crucial component of mentoring partnerships. The mentee must have faith that the mentor will offer accurate and sincere advice and have their best interests in mind. They must rely on one another to keep secret information private because the corporate sector may be fiercely competitive. They demonstrate two ways to build trust in these relationships by keeping their word and communicating often.

"It's crucial to make a sensible choice when picking a mentor. They ought to be someone you like and strive to emulate. Having said that, all effective mentors possess a number of traits."

- Your mentor should, at the very least, have more experience than you have and a successful track record. Seek mentors who are sincere, kind, original, and truthful. You need someone who will tell you the truth as well as someone who cares about your professional development. Sometimes you need a reality check or some constructive criticism, and other times you just need a high five or a pat on the back. All of those things may be given by a wise mentor.

> *"A wonderful mentor is someone whose traits make up a far better version of who you picture yourself to become."*

- Similar to your own values. Although productive mentoring relationships don't always have to be in the same field, a mentor in the same business area may better grasp your company's difficulties and worries. Maybe more significantly, is the leadership style.
- Make sure the mentor and you have comparable leadership and management values. Prior to beginning a mentoring relationship, it is essential to understand your leadership style. You may then contact yourself with the proper guidance only after that.

> *"Being a mentor is a means to further develop your leadership abilities since true leaders become excellent mentors."*

It is easy to get into the habit of relying heavily on your mentor without providing anything in return as a mentee. Even if your mentor could be delighted to provide you with guidance, it's crucial to consider methods to express your gratitude and be accessible to your mentor.

How to make a mentor-mentee connection more valuable?

Even if they might not have much to give their mentors, young professionals can nonetheless show them respect and gratitude. When you follow through on your commitments and keep your mentor in the loop, you can be a terrific mentee to your mentor. Chances are, if they're the perfect fit for you, they'll enjoy sharing information. Tell them you appreciate them, and don't waste your time.

It's essential to at the very least demonstrate that you value the connection by respecting your mentor's counsel and time. For instance, you could show up early or change your schedule to make a meeting more convenient for your mentorur.

Except when you want people to take after you, self-love is never a bad thing. Such self-love may exist among some mentors.It is best to exercise caution and quickly cut ties with anyone you believe to be a possible mentor who wishes to mould you into their image and render you completely dependent on them. They tend to be brash and like to hold the reins of your professional life. But no genuine mentor enjoys leading you down that route because they realise they can only offer advice, not direction.

- A mentor has a solid understanding of the best course of action to pursue and what you need to have in place in order to achieve your objective since they have extensive expertise.
- They are well-versed in the paperwork required to launch a company, how to grow your personnel while

still making money, how to organise your teams, and how to create a solid company culture from the start.

> *"A mentor who finds methods for you to improve in areas inside and beyond the office is irreplaceable. The difference between a mentor and a cheerleader is based on this quality."*

- A mentor is familiar with your professional development, preferred courses, and strengths and limitations. They can spot the holes that must be plugged in order to accomplish your objectives. On the other hand, a cheerleader is solely there to encourage. While a mentor occasionally serves as a cheerleader, their goal is to help you improve, not merely feel better.

How to approach your mentoring relationship with initiative?

Find someone you aspire to be like and who can assist you in areas where you lack knowledge and abilities. The exchange of experiences and tales led to my most memorable mentor encounters, and eventually the mentee could teach the mentor new skills. You want to foster an atmosphere where you're sharing your expertise with others.

> *"The goal of finding a mentor is to develop your career and get important insights. Only if you take control of your circumstances is this feasible."*

In 2021, I went to a conference with my mentees. We only had time to attend two sessions, but afterward, we researched additional topics we were curious about and spoke about what we had learnt. After the event, have a briefing with each other to make sure you're using the knowledge you've learned rather than merely ticking a box.

If both parties are receptive and dedicated to the process, someone with less professional experience can mentor someone with more expertise. Like mentees, mentors might come from the same department but have varying levels of education and experience.

> *"According to the research, 43% of office workers think that having a sense of value is more essential than receiving financial rewards like bonus plans and health insurance. This shows a noticeable change in how workers see the place of work in their lives."*

A mentor is there to help you grow on your path, whether you desire one to advance in your work or are someone who suffers with soft skills. Numerous studies have demonstrated the amazing advantages of mentoring others, including the expansion of one's network and increased chances of advancement within an organisation.

Due to the growing number of organisations implementing mentoring programmes to advance the learning, professional development, and skills of their workers, we are now witnessing a sharp rise in the number of people seeking mentors. I've gathered the most recent mentoring statistics list, some of which you probably weren't aware of, in light of the constantly growing need for mentoring and the wealth of data that is currently accessible.

"Mentees who have mentors are promoted five times more frequently than non-mentees."

When it comes down to it, everyone must be proactive in advancing and growing their own careers. Find out what a mentor is and how to choose the right one to assist you in achieving your professional objectives.

"A mentor is an established professional who provides informal advice to a less seasoned employee."

The mentee's needs should always come first, and the mentor should adjust their mentoring approach accordingly. Find a seasoned mentor in your network or sector whose management and leadership principles you appreciate. Whatever level of your career you are at, personal and professional growth are vital. However, if you have little professional experience, you could occasionally feel disoriented when navigating your career path and sector.

"A mentor is a person who has years or decades of practical experience in your area and can help you develop your professional abilities and acquire priceless lessons."

Do you want to acquire some useful skills if this is your first time managing a team? Are you a novice cybersecurity professional attempting to make a decision on how to further your career? All of these are good arguments for mentoring, but you must be specific.

Helping you carry out your objective is the main responsibility of a mentor. They can assist you with challenging questions, lead you in the direction of necessary resources, and work to keep you responsible. And while both the mentor and the mentee share responsibility for making course adjustments or initiating difficult dialogues when things aren't going as planned, I believe the mentor bears the lion's share of that burden.

In a professional mentoring relationship, an experienced person (the mentor) shares their knowledge, skills, and wisdom with a less experienced person (the mentee) while also developing their own mentoring abilities. Professional guidance may be provided to the mentee while still maintaining a cordial and encouraging connection with the mentor. The mentee's requirements should always come first, and a mentor should adjust their mentoring approach accordingly. You may benefit from a mentor whether you are establishing an organisation, launching a career, or already have some business expertise.

> "*A mentor may act as a sounding board at pivotal times in your career. They can offer career management advice that you might not be able to receive from other sources, an insider's view of the sector, and introductions to important industry contacts.*"

We need a tale to make sense of the happenings in our lives since humans are natural storytellers. Mentoring couples that regularly reflect on their beginnings, progress, and future goals will develop the fortitude necessary to overcome obstacles. To communicate progress, pairs should establish goals, check in often, and establish a public or semi-public forum. Companies need to deliberately encourage digital counterparts in a remote workplace, even though similar forums may have occurred informally in the office. It is possible to encourage a culture of celebration by sharing films and photos of victories and participating actively in public and private internet forums.

You'll discover that your new informal mentee is just waiting to be invited to participate, and you'll instantly have a connection for upcoming opportunities. Although finding a mentor may be a natural process, it's important to take the initiative and position yourself for a fruitful mentorship connection. Here are a few tips:

Decide what you want your career to be like. In order to choose a mentor, you must first decide what you want to get out of your profession. Because possibilities and unexpected routes may present themselves, you don't need to map out your whole professional path. Instead, outline your short-term goals to provide you with a clear way forward.

> *"A mentor is a dependable counsellor who gives you the resources, direction, and criticism you need to succeed in your work. A classmate, manager, friend, supervisor, family member, school alumnus, or other person might be a mentor."*

In order to help you navigate your career and accomplish your goals, mentors with the necessary expertise and abilities can provide guidance on your particular function or industry. A mentor, though, is neither a celebrity nor someone you simply follow online. They must be familiar with your life and dependable enough to provide you with advice over time. Having stated that, a mentorship relationship may continue for a few months or for many years.

Someone you can look up to is a mentor. You admire them for their creative output, moral principles, and distinctive character.This might involve discussing problems that happen at work (such as salary negotiations, promotions, difficulties with a colleague or manager, quitting a job, or getting let go).

> *"The mentor-mentee connection gains enthusiasm and velocity when it is imbued with a distinct sense of purpose, which helps to cement the relationship. Without it, mentorship can develop into lovely friendships but won't aid in an employee's goal-achieving."*

Examine the details of mentoring, including what a mentor actually does, what a mentee accomplishes, and why mentoring is important for a successful career, workplace culture, and more. The more time you spend together, the more a mentor gets to know your learning preferences, personality, and long-term objectives.

> *"When the mentor and mentee are the appropriate fit, mentoring relationships succeed."*

Reach out to someone you feel familiar with who can serve as a terrific resource and a neutral sounding board. Look at your network of professionals. Former coworkers, professors, teachers, colleagues from a different department, persons you met through an internship programme, and friends from your family can all be included in your professional circle.

Look for people who are familiar with your field and position. In order to acquire advice on things like new projects, certifications, and training you need to progress ahead, as well as how to handle office politics inside your firm or organisation, find someone who has a general understanding of your present function and sector. When you're prepared to contact someone, it's crucial to keep things informal. According to me, you should treat a prospective mentor the same way you would a prospective friend; your connection will grow with time. Don't push things; maintain your calm. Lessons and suggestions will surface over time.

To locate a mentor, specify your professional objectives, choose your role models, focus on specific individuals in your network and sector, and establish informal but potential-rich professional connections.

Why you ought to think about seeking out a mentor?

You can gain a fresh perspective from a seasoned professional through mentoring. Whether you've just begun your first job or are halfway through your career, learning from someone more experienced is a priceless business opportunity. It's easy to lose sight of the present when we fall into the daily routine of professional life.

> *"A mentor may be a useful resource for young, aspiring entrepreneurs and individuals who are new to the business world. The advantages of working with a mentor are numerous."*

Our viewpoint may be reset by a mentor, allowing us to view our professional development and advancement from a fresh angle. The first step in choosing a mentor is to put in the effort and establish a personal reputation for success. You may position yourself to network with more seasoned business professionals who will see your skills and wish to assist you in growing by concentrating on your job and career.

As a result, they can provide you with advice that is more pertinent to you and includes context. Conversely, brief mentor-mentee partnerships are excellent for addressing certain issues or obstacles. For instance, while looking for a job, you may have an informational interview and meet a mentor. If everything goes well, they could recommend you or put you in touch with the recruiting manager.

You may develop and widen your network through both short-term and long-term mentorships. You will probably have both kinds of mentors during your career. Keep in mind few top mentor qualities as you search for your go-to people for professional advice.

You may be familiar with the concept of a board of directors for an organisation, but you may also establish your own "board of advisers" or mentors since often just one isn't enough. But to do that, you must be clear about what you expect from your mentor. If you want industry insights, reach out to someone outside your place of employment if you want impartial counsel, and if you want entrepreneurial assistance, get in touch with someone who has had experiences you can benefit from. One may not be enough, as I already stated.

However, there is no doubt that mentoring is significant and may have a significant impact by offering valuable and honest criticism. This collaborative partnership for knowledge exchange benefits more than just the mentor-mentee relationship. When mentoring relationships are successful, businesses benefit as well.

> *"The goal and aim of the mentoring relationship must be understood by both sides. The mentor and mentee should also express their expectations for the relationship."*

Find a mentor who possesses the expertise and experience you would like to acquire, and learn from them. Just keep in mind that every person's path is different, so when taking their advice into account, do what feels right for you. Your mentor must have relevant skills and knowledge. This quality generally matters the most out of all the qualities to look for in a mentor.

It takes time to build enough trust to discuss difficulties. Find a mentor who respects this period and doesn't pressure you to provide sensitive material straight away. The objective is to develop an honest, respectful, and expert connection. Regardless of your age or experience, the one thing you must take into account is the relationships your mentor has.

- Do they own a robust network?
- Do they have connections to key figures in your field?
- Do they intend to present you or suggest you for a position?

Someone you know who is an excellent listener and gives insightful counsel can make a wonderful mentor for you. The single best method to recruit a mentor is to establish a reputation as someone who is teachable, interested, driven, talented, and, above all, well-balanced and reliable.

> *"Finding a mentor entails understanding how to do proper follow-up, contributing to your mentor's life and work, and taking the initiative to advance your career."*

Any worker at any level of their career may benefit from these teachings, but young professionals who are just starting out in their careers or lack the necessary experience to advance are especially in need of them.

> *"A mentor is a role model—someone who has paved the way for success after having been in your position."*

It's important to comprehend how a mentor-mentee connection works. According to me the relationship between a mentor and a mentee need not necessarily be intense or formal. It is preferable to concentrate on sustaining the professional connection and gaining as much knowledge as you can.

Despite the fact that it might be a daunting procedure, here's how you can find a mentor for yourself. Everyone, from job seekers to those in senior positions, has occasionally felt the need for a mentor's counsel, and there's nothing wrong with it. That in no way implies that you are unable to make independent judgments. With a little bit of drive, direction, and understanding, we can sometimes do far better. Anyone wanting to manage their professional path at any level might benefit from mentors because they act as catalysts in this respect. Despite the fact that looking for a mentor might be frightening, here's how to do it effectively. You could also get a reality check from this.

Finding a mentor who appreciates that things happen in life, people become sick, and priorities change is thus preferable. They have to be prepared to demonstrate their humanity and provide advice in a way that appeals to you personally.

Sometimes it may seem that your colleague is the ideal candidate to serve as your mentor, or it may be someone from outside your workplace, a member of your professional network, or even a member of your family who can help you make sense of things when you're confused. In the end, it should be someone whose output you appreciate, whose work ethics you respect, and whom you honestly believe can further your career.

Mentors with high emotional intelligence pay attention to you and show empathy. They are aware of your vulnerability and capacity for error. Furthermore, they help you feel at ease discussing both the positive and negative events that are happening in your life. Every professional relationship needs empathy, but empathy is especially crucial in mentorship.

Discard the conventional idea of a "mentor." Don't daydream about having a mentor who will show up and tell you they have your back. You must take the initiative. It's possible that your mentor is an older or more experienced person than you. Put an end to your pigeonhole thinking.

A mentor's usage when if:

- You want to pick up knowledge from a more seasoned expert in your industry.
- You seek suggestions and direction on how to advance your career within your company or sector.
- You wish to expand your network of industry experts from whom you can learn.

- You are seeking strategies to successfully manage the difficulties particular to the culture of your firm.
- Your objectives are not time-bound, and you have the freedom to develop an ongoing, mutually beneficial relationship with your mentor.
- You desire clarity on your life's true goals and the obstacles in your path.
- Instead of resolving and moving past the past, your major priorities revolve around creating a particular sort of future.
- You're looking for someone to hold you responsible for achieving your objectives.
- You believe that you are not reaching your full potential on the personal or professional front.
- You have a longing for a life that is more purposeful and satisfying.
- You think your prior experiences are preventing you from moving forward.
- You're displaying signs of anxiety, sadness, or another mental health issue.
- You are unable to move because of trauma or loss.
- You've been dealing with persistent emotional pain.
- You discover that you have a tendency to participate in unhappy partnerships.

There is no ideal method for finding a mentor, but there are a few factors to consider. Does this person currently hold, formerly hold, or have experience in the role or career path you wish to pursue? Do you share any traits that could allow you to get along better? Although it's not the most crucial element, it's wonderful to have a connection since it makes discussion easier. Look for people who are interested in your work and can serve as role models for you. However, you don't have to have mentors that look like you, which is a crucial caution.

"If you have a mentor, your career is undoubtedly moving forward. In addition, mentoring is a mutually beneficial relationship in which both mentors and mentees benefit. Every successful businessperson or entrepreneur will often have a mentor they look up to and learn from."

In my opinion, encouragement is the best gift we can provide to one another. For me, it is crucial to know that I am speaking with someone in this mentorship relationship who is intrigued by the central notion. I believe it would be far less intriguing if it were only about assisting me in moving on to the next stage.

Find a person that pushes you to grow. Humans naturally tend to feel more sympathetic toward those we have a lot in common with. When meeting new acquaintances, this could be useful, but not when looking for a mentor.

Find someone who possesses the qualities you lack. For example, finding someone who is confident and outspoken will be a good idea since, for example, you might not be excellent at networking because you're an introvert.

"Having a mentor will also help you get out of your rut because it's normal for you to develop patterns and a consistent strategy for handling particular situations. No matter what level of your job you are at, development is something that is advantageous."

Let me share a short story of Jivan who wants to improve himself as a leader, a new manager combines coaching and mentoring. Jivan just changed jobs to become a manager of software engineering. He had been an engineer for about seven years before this. He is having trouble in his new position since all the things that had previously helped him succeed in his job no longer seem to be working as well.

He felt considerably more productive and was able to complete tasks much more quickly before he was promoted to manager. In his new position, he must do tasks through other people, which appears to take significantly longer. While Jivan frequently feels the need to get in and start working right away, he is aware that this is not sustainable. Simply put, he is unable to meet the needs of every member of his team.

In order to overcome this obstacle, Jivan chooses to work with a mentor. Clarifying what Jivan genuinely wants—to be able to produce outcomes through his team without sacrificing quality or speed—is the first step in the mentoring process.

When Jivan's asks him about inspirational leaders in his company, he immediately thinks of a director who looks very skilled at inspiring others to produce top-notch outcomes. Jivan makes the decision to ask this director for mentorship. Before making the request, he does a lot of research and thinks carefully about the procedure.

Finally, Jivan succeeds in developing a mentorship relationship with this director, albeit it takes some time. Jivan always thinks carefully and strategically about how to use his mentor's time since he is aware of how busy the director is. He keeps meeting with his coach once a week to make sure he is moving toward his goals steadily. Working with a coach and mentor at the same time enables John to increase his effectiveness more quickly.

By providing suggestions for improvement and dispensing timely counsel, mentors assist you in developing both personally and professionally. But the capacity to concentrate on both your growth and their own sets the finest mentors apart. You want a mentor who has been in your shoes and can help you advance, of course.

"A mentor is a treasure if they invest time in growing personally and pushing themselves outside their comfort zones."

More and more, young professionals and new workers are exhorted—sometimes vehemently—to find a mentor! Strong mentoring relationships have the power to alter people and whole organisations, according to four decades of study, which shows that the impacts of mentoring may be significant and long-lasting. Businesses that keep and advance outstanding personnel, male and female, are more likely to succeed.

Do you have a mentor?

Walk the talk learning is a lifelong process; one does not suddenly arrive at a point when they are the all-knowing mentor with nothing else to learn. If you are both a mentor and a mentee, your mentoring efforts will be more effective and well-received. Telling your mentee how you've benefitted from mentors in the past and now can help you demonstrate to them how much you believe in the mentoring process.

How to interact with a mentor in a positive way?

Fix times for routine check-ups. After your initial meeting and talk with a potential mentor, carefully consider how and when to follow up. If they agree to continue the conversation, schedule follow-up appointments on your calendar. It's up to you how frequently you communicate with your mentor, but the main objective is ongoing, long-term understanding. That could include calling or meeting for coffee once every three months, or perhaps twice a year.

Make use of social media. Social media gives mentees the chance to communicate with mentors on a regular basis without feeling rushed. Use LinkedIn and Twitter for light topics like amusing articles, recommended books, significant business news, etc. Through social media, mentees may gently remind their mentors how much they appreciate the relationship. But be careful not to nudge too often, or you could come across as forceful. Keep important communications for face-to-face meetings only. Never discuss important career topics on social media or over email. Keep that for face-to-face encounters only.

Think beyond the box in terms of 'OK, I'll meet you at your office' or 'Can we FaceTime?' to obtain that engagement if their schedule is full. You should not limit yourself to sending emails. Use traditional mail. A significant way to communicate with your mentor is via mail. Showing your mentor that you appreciate their counsel and presence in your life with a thank-you message or holiday card may go a long way.

Active listening, which is more crossover, means being receptive and actively listening ensures that you benefit from the conversation. Mentoring shouldn't seem like a chore, so it's a good idea to leave when that happens.

Keep things simple and unhurried while dealing with a mentor. There is frequently something to learn from someone who is further along in their career. Being receptive to whatever lesson or message it may be is the key. Choose the best individual to advance your career. You need to find someone who can assist, whether you're aiming for a particular leadership position, seeking to improve your abilities, or just trying to expand your professional network. You'll likely wait an eternity if you wait for a senior manager to come looking for you. Instead, you should look for guidance that will aid in your goal-achieving. When used effectively, mentoring may be a strong and effective strategy for career advancement.

- Discover fresh approaches to stand out inside your company.
- Establish precise and practical growth objectives.
- Locate and cultivate connections with significant sponsors.
- Pay it forward and add value to senior advisers and mentors.
- Assess your progress toward achieving your career objectives.

The end aim is to establish a relationship with someone who inspires you and with whom you can both engage and influence. Your ideal transformational mentor should be someone who likes to have meaningful conversations with you over giving you quick answers so that you may both learn and develop.

> "*A wonderful mentoring relationship can be the result of a variety of factors. In my opinion, mentoring has become even more crucial to helping people learn and evolve in our modern context of hybrid and remote work.*"

You may even start to help them if you can grasp their priorities and aspirations. Consider this as a relational currency investment—a conscious effort to invest in people, which frequently results in their appreciation, reciprocation, and eagerness to return the favour.

Above all, they ought to make you reevaluate your presumptions and statements and sharpen your future-focused thinking. You have to have both individual and group meetings with your mentees. As much as feasible, objectives, passions, and project work should be compatible. Everyone begins the mentoring experience with a goal in mind in this manner.

What advice would you offer to a worker seeking a mentor?

I believe that establishing a framework is the best thing they can do. It is the responsibility of the employee to be clear about their objectives, to set them, and to make sure that they communicate them to their mentor. The mentee has to be trustworthy, accountable, and aware of what they want from the connection from the outset. The mentor should then periodically check in with the mentee to see how they're doing, ensure that they're accomplishing those goals, and to find out what they may be doing differently to make the relationship better.

There are many factors, but it's a success when both the mentor and the mentee are learning. A strong mentoring relationship can also encourage the development of other relationships. Sometimes a mentoring connection may develop into a sponsorship relationship, which we know we need more of as we advance in our jobs. The goal is to mentor those relationships while you're in a mentoring relationship and hope that they will develop so that you can then continue them into a sponsoring relationship.

What must mentees, and even mentors, avoid doing in this circumstance?

I believe that speaking up is important. Don't assume there isn't much work for you to do just because the mentor is leaving it up to you as the mentee. As I have stated, you must own that connection. You need to establish the relationship's tone, purpose, and open lines of communication. The mentor must also be ready and open to discuss their past experiences, including how they could apply to what their mentee is doing now. A new career or sector might be scary to enter. As workers negotiate The Great Resignation, mentoring takes on greater significance.

Closeout Take the time to wrap up if you are a member of a formal mentoring relationship or if a set number of mentoring meetings has been agreed upon. This is the time for both parties to pause and express gratitude.

- What could I change to make this experience more satisfying?
- What did you think was the most priceless?
- What was the most satisfying?
- What do you most appreciate?
- How is this going for you?
- What has proved useful?
- What remained?

It should be a question that one (or both) parties asks at every meeting. Despite how difficult it may feel, starting an evaluative dialogue can help you both maintain the relationship. Mentors and mentees should express their gratitude to one another in a straightforward and concise manner. From your experience, be precise about the knowledge and benefits you obtained from your experience. A gratifying and even life-changing experience can be provided by mentoring for both the mentor and the mentee. It is one of the most important things a person can do to advance in their professional and professional lives. Although it requires time and dedication, the work is definitely worth it. It benefits your career, whether you are the mentor or the mentee.

There is at least one mentor that counts in every person's life—someone whose perspectives inspire transformation and whose impact lasts. It may be a teacher whose expertise sparks a new enthusiasm. a family member whose knowledge helps us avoid catastrophic errors or supports our most audacious aspirations.

- A professional whose education inspires us to go above and beyond what we had anticipated.
- A leader who inspires bravery or strength.
- A companion who recognises and supports our untapped talents.
- Someone may be seated next to us in a kitchen, workplace, or classroom. a coworker of ours at a studio, gym, or laboratory.
- Someone thousands of kilometres or even abroad.
- Even someone we only know from reading news articles, books, historical accounts, or the elegance of a piece of art.

Recall how our parents read us bedtime tales and how, even as adults, we still light the nightstand lamp and engage in a little reading time? Your mentors are your guides, and they have plenty of stories they'd love to share with you. They want you to benefit from their experiences, both good and bad, throughout their career. Look for solutions to the issues they raise. Ask questions and make sure you leave your coffee-table conversation or online discussions with at least one takeaway. Above all, keep in mind that you can always find a mentor, so why deprive yourself? The only genuine indicator of a learner is someone who tries to develop via both their own and other people's experiences. Additionally, be sure to thank them for all of their assistance and guidance because your relationship should not be one of parasite and host but rather one of mutual benefit.

> *"Mentors actually know the best since they have dealt with challenges that you have not yet encountered. They support your growth and assist you in finding your abilities. Nevertheless, they frequently make no big demands in return from their mentees and even endure personal annoyance during the mentoring session."*

Holding one to four monthly sessions is an operational norm for mentoring. The sessions, which can last up to two hours, might be used to discuss a particular subject. There is no need for you to bring any graphs, charts, or other graphics.

The mentoring session is a conversation, not a bargaining session, so it can take place anywhere—even outside on the cafeteria patio. It is not about looking well or leaving a good first impression with anyone. Instead, it focuses on talking about issues that are directly relevant to the duties involved in a professional setting. For their overall development, mentees can even discuss their own aspirations with mentors if necessary. Both sides must agree on how much the mentor should be paid for their respective time commitments. Mentorship is, in theory, not commercial consulting and is thus exempt from professional fees. Organisations must realise that, in addition to receiving personal fulfilment from assisting, mentors also get paid.

"Mentorship encourages the growth and advancement of employees, which helps with retention."

On the recruitment front, taking part in undergraduate mentoring creates talent pipelines and opens doors to students who are frequently shut out of standard hiring processes, such as those from community colleges. If hiring errors and inadequate staff assistance were always expensive, the stakes are now even higher. We can prevent both by mentoring.

In order to help individuals through difficult times and to fortify ties within an organisation, it is crucial to connect with people and give their lives meaning via rapport and a clear sense of purpose. While it makes sense to most people that mentoring will aid new hires in their careers, the influence on individuals doing the mentoring is frequently disregarded.

Finally, remember your official or unofficial mentee will enjoy reading your email when they check their inbox. Send them resources that have been valuable to your profession. Tell your mentee how this tool has benefited your profession or kept you abreast of current events. So that they may participate in how choices are made or discussions about certain issues develop, CC them on an email thread.

"When it comes to business, your mentors are the ones that kindle the fire in your hearts. They inspire you, help you through difficult times, and direct your paths. Learning from those who have gone before you is an excellent way to avoid making costly mistakes."- Dr. Amit Das

The Powerful Benefits Of Mentorship

"Mentoring is a brain to pick, an ear to listen, and a push in the right direction." — John Crosby

An excellent mentor is willing to include you in their inner circle because they have worked hard to build strong relationships with others throughout the years. This might aid in growing your network and opening up.

Having a mentor can help professionals in their early careers gain a thorough understanding of their future career path. Since they have more experience than you have, your mentor has certainly made a number of mistakes along the way to where they are now. Therefore, by seeking your mentor's professional advice, you may become aware of any potential hazards in your career path and prevent them.

"*A mentor may become an ally and become aware of the challenges you encounter by working with you.*"

Experiences with mentoring are quite important. Regardless of your sector, serving as a mentor will improve both your leadership and your teaching. In many cases, mentoring aids in formulating a strategy for fixing an issue, but you still need to put in the work. Unfortunately, employees still have to self-advocate excessively.

How a mentor may help you advance professionally the quickest?

Although mentoring may seem to be the newest buzzword these days, it has really been around for a very long time. Nowadays, there is a big increase in the need for mentorship, whether it be from young entrepreneurs seeking assistance with their ventures, working professionals seeking to progress in their professions, or students deciding on their future paths. As straightforward as it may seem, mentorship has a significant impact on how a person's career and professional development are shaped. Professionals may lose their focus or aren't aware of the goals they are pursuing. In this situation, mentoring is a potent professional tool that supports desired development and directs mentee toward a more important course.

A mentee seeks someone to provide direction as they work through any professional obstacles or conundrums they may be encountering. Furthermore, mentors' primary goal is to assist their mentees in realising their full potential and succeeding more in life (another goal, similar to mentors', is to experience immense satisfaction when they see their mentee succeed as a result of their inputs).

A great way to establish deep ties with others at your organisation is to volunteer as a mentor. You can help one or more of your coworkers achieve their career objectives while also improving your understanding of your organisation, developing your leadership abilities, and advancing your own professional growth by offering advice and support to one or more of them.

A mentor can assist their mentee in expanding their professional network. The mentor can introduce the mentee to prospective prospects or people who can assist them when they identify their career or personal objectives. These relationships can be helpful for job progress because the mentor often has more expertise in the field or a more senior position. By mentoring someone else, you will develop your ability to explain and communicate your thoughts clearly, which is crucial for the advancement of your career.

When done with intention, mentoring is a powerful tool for creating a feeling of community among coworkers. It has been demonstrated to aid in employee advancement, growth, and retention.

> *"In actuality, 97% of those who have a mentor think they are useful. Additionally, mentees are promoted five times as frequently as non-mentees."*

These investigations might take a lot of time, so be careful to surround yourself with individuals who can constructively challenge your beliefs. To make room for individuals who actually push you ahead, you may need to withdraw from the more transactional professional ties you may have developed. However, once you meet the right person, it will have been well worth it.

A formal mentoring programme is a terrific way to encourage interaction and mutual learning among your staff members. Because mentor-mentee relationships are informal, knowledge may be shared more effectively, allowing a business to capitalise on the expertise and abilities of its own personnel. For instance, Google sponsors "Summer of Code," a worldwide initiative that matches students from more than 100 nations with various mentors to help them develop their talents and gain real-world software development experience.

When someone gets an idea, they might discuss it with or test it out with a mentor. With the aid of their pertinent expertise and experience, the mentor can offer objective guidance or recommendations. These insights help the mentee decide whether to go with the concept or abandon it and what measures to take. Similarly, a mentor may assist people with day-to-day issues like conflict at work by listening to them and offering advice.

There are several advantages to mentoring. According to research, effective mentoring may help people achieve higher job success, including promotions, increases, and more chances. Employee engagement, retention, and knowledge sharing are all better in organisations that value mentorship.

> "In fact, 71% of Fortune 500 businesses now provide mentorship programmes to their staff since it has been shown to be so useful."

The fundamental advantage of mentoring is that it creates a framework of understanding and clear guidelines. This assures the efficacy of the partnership and the quality of the process. A mentor can help map out your SMART goals. These are objectives that you would like your business to achieve within a set time. You can set your SMART goals and your mentor will hold you accountable for every milestone. These individuals frequently have their own mentors. They often strive to continually improve themselves and are lifelong learners. They not only follow their own hobbies, but they also support your objectives and innovation.

> *"It is impossible to emphasise the value of having a good mentor. A good mentor will encourage you to overcome obstacles, urge you to grow, broaden your perspective, and most importantly, a good mentor does not pass judgement. In the workplace, mentoring increases employee engagement and retention rates and provides a secure atmosphere for learning."*

When faced with difficult decisions or attempting to solve business obstacles, mentors may serve as a sounding board. Sometimes all you need to get over a challenge is a new point of view. The majority of mentors have a wealth of knowledge in their sector and can provide excellent insights into the markets, trends, and industries currently in existence. Not only may they provide support during difficult times, but they can also contribute some original ideas.

Mentors may assist you build your network by introducing you to other experts. Never undervalue the influence of a strong network. It assists in presenting new business prospects, recommendations for your company, a new channel for locating suppliers, and a platform to promote your brand.

> *"According to the American Society for Training and Development, 75% of executives who were questioned attribute their successful careers to their mentors."*

Companies may increase employee engagement by developing mentoring programmes for their skilled staff. By encouraging mentees to update their abilities, mentors help them feel at home in the company, foster a culture of learning, and build connections with them. Increasing workers' pleasure at work Employees who participate in mentoring programmes report having a higher level of work satisfaction because they believe that their company is invested in their professional growth.

How can someone else help us be the most powerful versions of ourselves?

In the hybrid workplace of today, mentoring is crucial. And while the structure or manner of the mentoring relationship between the mentor and the mentee may have changed, the core objectives and benefits have remained constant. Sharing information and talents amongst people who want and need it most has the potential to unleash immense power.

A structured mentorship programme enables mentors and mentees to create a connection that is fruitful and advantageous to everyone involved by establishing checkpoints and structure. Beyond the limitations of casual mentoring, the relationship is elevated by the structure and responsibility given by official programmes, such as set goals, mentor/mentee training, and a formalised communication channel.

A structured programme can also foster more mentorship ties, especially with persons (workers and students) who are typically underserved by informal mentoring.

Mentorship is important since it may take place anywhere and in any style, manner, or setting. It may occur in a variety of places, including the workplace and educational institutions. Professional associations are another way to form connections. Additionally, some networks have informal mentorship ties.

Mentorship programmes are sometimes designed to assist with career development and assistance. Mentoring can occasionally help in attempts to promote diversity and inclusion. Mentorship can also introduce young people to compassionate, active role models. There is a reason why 71% of Fortune 500 businesses have mentorship programmes.

Organisations are aware that substandard hires and attrition both increase expenses for the business. A mentorship program, by fostering a culture of sharing and care, may be a critical enabler in their increased retention efforts.

"According to data from the Emerging Workforce research, 35% of survey respondents who weren't enrolled in any mentorship programmes considered changing employment within a year."

This demonstrates how mentorship programmes may increase an employee's loyalty. These programmes' benefits are holistic in nature, assisting both the mentor and mentee as well as the entire business. With the help of these programmes, mentees may network and improve their social skills inside the company. This not only boosts their self-confidence but also gives them a better understanding of the culture and principles of the company.

Even while these figures are positive, it's crucial to keep in mind that mentoring is not a magic wand that guarantees success. Effective mentoring does involve work, and developing fruitful mentoring relationships calls for certain abilities, sensibilities, and structure from both the mentor and the mentee. When both sides are committed to making things work, success results. When the three essential parts are combined in the best possible way, success results.

Why is mentoring is so valuable?

Because it gives workers the chance to advance in their careers, become more proficient in their jobs, and position themselves for future advancement chances, mentoring is crucial. Offering these opportunities is essential for businesses that wish to draw in, keep, and engage people.

What do mentoring programmes aim to achieve?

The goal of mentoring is to develop by drawing on the wisdom and experience of someone who has gone before you. The best approach to quickening your growth is to do it. In this chapter, I cover every aspect of mentoring, including its advantages, characteristics of effective mentors, applications in the workplace, and how to start a mentorship programme.

How mentees are going to get benefited by mentorship programme?

The following are some crucial advantages for mentors:

- Beneficial mentoring equips mentees with fresh knowledge, institutional insight, and encouragement, in addition to providing them with new skills. Become more effective employees: Mentors' feedback and direction can enhance job effectiveness.
- Developing your communication skills can help you become more capable of speaking in the future, just as your mentor may pick up some communication tips from you.

- When a less experienced employee encounters a scenario or issue that they are unfamiliar with or for which they are unable to find a solution, a mentor can serve as a sounding board. The mentee gains knowledge from the mentor's experience by being paired with a more seasoned employee.
- The majority of mentees want mentors who can assist them in improving their job chances. The mentor can assist the employee in realising their full potential or cultivating an entrepreneurial mentality in the workplace by offering advice and direction.
- One study found that taking part in mentoring might result in pay raises and promotions, while another found that it could boost work satisfaction.
- One benefit of having a mentor at a new job is that they may aid in your quicker integration into the workplace environment.

> *"Employees who take part in a mentoring programme are more knowledgeable about workplace procedures, rules, and expectations than non-participants. Building inclusive workplaces depends on this."*

As before, you can pick up some tips from your mentor to change the way you look at things. The more seasoned worker should be well-versed in the organisation as well as any programmes or training that a mentee may take advantage of to assist in achieving their objectives.

- The mentor can provide knowledge gained through experience, facts, and guidelines from the workplace that will assist the mentee achieve in the long term.

- Your career can get the boost it needs from a dependable mentor, launching it on the road to success.
- Mentors have insightful suggestions that might advance your professional life. They can serve as a "sounding board" for new concepts and aid in decision-making.
- They may also assist you in developing more effective methods to apply your natural talents and teach you the ones you need to function inside your firm, allowing you to swiftly shed the training wheels and advance in your profession.
- You will practise and improve your communication abilities much more quickly with this frequent conversation.

For information and ideas to be shared, there must be some communication between the mentor and the mentee. Learn to see things from a different perspective by working with someone who is less experienced than you and, as a result, does not necessarily have the same perspective on things as you. Over time, this could help you increase your capacity for creative problem solving. An increase in personal pleasure might emerge from seeing your mentee succeed as a direct result of your advice. It will improve both your overall job happiness and your sense of fulfilment.

In traditional mentoring, the mentee is typically a novice or a less seasoned professional than the mentor, who is typically a highly seasoned expert. The mentor possesses the skills and information necessary to pass them on to the mentee. He is a skilled active listener who can provide constructive criticism that can advance the mentee's career. Even though it could look like a one-way information transfer, it typically isn't. The mentees, who are frequently young professionals, typically have far more in-depth technological expertise, which they may impart to their mentors.

There are qualities and sensitivities that make for a good mentee, just as there are qualities that make for a successful mentor. Being a good mentor is the best way to guarantee that the connection has a healthy, meaningful existence. This is crucial because mentees must keep in mind that mentors are doing this out of the kindness of their hearts.

Mentees should be committed to developing their skills and being professional and results-oriented.

> *"One who doesn't listen to other people's opinions will eventually end up on the wrong road. A mentor enables you to recognise your own faults and bravely address them. We are able to follow our chosen route through to the very end because of the relationship between mentor and mentees."*

Hopefully, the statements above will motivate you to seek out the best mentor. If you choose the appropriate mentor, they will undoubtedly have a big impact on your life. We begin the process of following and learning the moment we are born. Typically, parents serve as our initial mentors.

> *"We have an inbuilt propensity to allow other people to inspire us and encourage us to actively pursue our aspirations."*

The most effective instructors have and always will be those who are passionate lifelong learners. Which would you prefer: a person with a closed mind because they believe they already know everything, or a somebody with an open mind because they are constantly seeking to learn more? Clearly stating their requirements, objectives, and professional ambitions mentoring isn't like talking aimlessly in therapy. The mentoring agenda is created by the mentees, thus they must be specific about what they intend to gain from mentoring.

Essential Tips For Mentees:

The relationship between a mentor and a mentee is reciprocal. Mentors can benefit from mentees' criticism and fresh viewpoints as they develop their own leadership capacities. A mentee's job will vary, much like a mentor's, but some essential tasks include:

When you have someone to look up to, you will have the courage to make important job decisions and create plans to advance your career. It's a fantastic opportunity to take advantage of a mentorship programme if your company or place of employment offers one. Make use of these mentoring quotes to become motivated and inspired to locate your mentor and to value the one you already have.

- A mentee may stretch and move beyond their comfort zone, take chances, and show up honestly when a secure and trusting environment is established.
- Don't merely discuss your goals; really work for them. Accept the power of screen sharing, which encourages cooperation and is excellent for visual learners. Put mentees in control instead of giving in to the desire to always share; mentors will observe how mentees are doing and may even pick up some new skills.
- The mentee can seek assistance from their mentor when they are having trouble completing a task or achieving a goal.

- They may be inspired to keep going ahead in the face of obstacles by this support. In order to create confidence in their mentee, a mentor might also recognise and highlight their qualities.

  "A mentee who exudes confidence is less likely to give up on their objectives."

- Determine your career and establish workable business objectives.
- Recognise what you need to learn to achieve your objectives.
- Adopt a professional attitude.
- Treat your mentorship like a professional friendship. Be relaxed and kind and avoid embarrassing inquiries like, "Will you be my mentor?"
- Utilise your professional network to find a mentor. Your professional network may already include a mentor who offers guidance in a variety of ways. A little effort is all that's required to develop that connection into a lasting partnership.
- Actively As you are listening throughout the meeting, make notes on any topics you wish to learn more about.
- Ask the question if it relates to the theme of your current conversation; if not, use it as a springboard for your next one. By doing so, you are both able to get the most out of the meeting and are also given ideas for future discussions.
- Willing to investigate other avenues and viewpoints, be vulnerable, and seek for assistance. Mentees need to be open to learning and trying out new things. Nobody who is not willing to learn wants to get advice from a

mentor! Mentees must be able to ask for, receive, and act upon criticism, even "constructive" input.

- Be accountable and responsible for yourself. Mentors want to see progress and development. Do what you say you're going to do when you make a commitment. It won't work in a mentoring relationship to watch from the sidelines.

- Mentees must be able, willing, and prepared to meet often. Because it takes time for relationships to grow, mentees must also be dedicated to keeping their half of the contract.

- If you're a young professional just starting out in your career and don't already have one who can guide you in the proper direction, get a mentor as soon as you can.

- Consider yourself a serious mentee; prepare. It is ideal to have a purpose for your meeting with a mentor before you ask for their time, and when you do, come prepared with questions. Both sides value their time, and planning is the secret to a fruitful mentoring relationship.

- Planning and preparation are needed to prepare a subject and questions for each meeting, but doing so will help you make the most of the time available.

- If your company offers mentoring, discuss it with your manager when you first start working there. You may also brainstorm options with your boss. Your boss will be knowledgeable about individuals who might be a good fit for you individually and who would be willing to take on a mentee.

- Being attentive Mentees may demonstrate their appreciation for the time and effort mentors put in by being punctual, prepared for meetings, and professional.

- Making progress mentees should take the required action after receiving advice, recommendations, introductions, and the like, and be ready to provide updates at following sessions. That is, mentees should reply swiftly and responsibly whenever a mentor initiates contact between them and a member of their network via email. This maintains the positive rapport in the mentoring relationship and serves to affirm the mentor's efforts and effort.

However, mentees can at the very least express thanks and appreciation to their mentors for fostering their personal development. However, you could have trouble finding the correct phrases to use with your mentors. Perhaps your mentor has helped you at every stage of your journey to success.

"It's nice to be told what you're doing right, but it may be challenging to hear what needs to be changed or improved."

However, mentees should be honest in their responses to comments, both positive and negative, since this is ultimately helpful information meant to aid in growth and future success. They should also be ready to provide their mentors with the same direct criticism. This guarantees mutual learning between the two parties.

To become a better leader, a young professional combines coaching and counseling. Let me share a short story of Bipasa who is a young marketing specialist newly elevated to management, works for a sizable pharmaceutical business. She has a great commitment to, and is driven by, the goals of her company.

As this will be her first experience managing people, she is both excited and a little anxious at the possibility of leading a team. She seeks coaching because she wants to understand how to develop into a great leader.

It's important to maintain and manage a mentoring relationship. Because it is a joint business, both parties must actively participate in taking care of it. By using a few straightforward best practises, the odds of starting and maintaining a good mentoring relationship are increased: The alliance's design spend some time talking about how the relationship is structured. It's important for both sides to comprehend how a relationship develops. This entails talking about and stating issues like: Starting with establishing objectives, a timetable, and expectations to ensure that the mentee's goals are met as well as how both parties will be held responsible is the first step in the mentoring process.

It is up to the mentor to guide conversations and offer knowledge and resources that aid the mentee in achieving their goals after the program's objectives have been established.

- What are the objectives and responsibilities for each stakeholder in this experience?
- What kind of accountability does the mentee desire from the mentor?
- What kind of accountability does the mentor demand from the mentee?
- What are the criteria for providing and receiving feedback?
- What information may be shared and what cannot?
- What are the mentoring's guidelines?
- What is permitted and prohibited?

Learn about one another. A mentoring relationship takes time to build, just like any other kind of friendship. Like other relationships, it will develop more quickly and strongly if both sides put in the effort to get to know one another on a personal level. Avoid the urge to go right into career counselling and issue solutions. Establish trust by getting to know one another.

Bipasa discovers that she is quite skilled at forming connections with people and spotting them when she works with her coach and mentor. Bipasa discovers that she tends to shy away from confrontation, which might prevent her from having unpleasant yet crucial talks with her team.

Bipasa works with her coach and mentor to learn what aspects of confrontation make her uncomfortable and how she can get past these barriers since she is dedicated to improving her leadership effectiveness. With time and effort, Bipasa expands her leadership toolkit and gains the ability to handle challenging conversations at work.

However, Bipasa also learns via this process that her conflict avoidance is a result of some unresolved childhood trauma. She regrets this and tries to make up for the less than perfect connection she now has with her family. Because Bipasa is looking for closure to past events that have caused her mental suffering, her coach and mentor direct her to a counsellor. She can keep working with her coach and mentor to improve her leadership abilities, but it would be better if she sought out counselling to help her deal with her history. This example shows how coaching, mentoring, and counselling may be used in tandem depending on the requirements of the individual.

How mentors are going to get benefited by mentorship programme?

The following are some crucial advantages for mentors:

- Mentors will gain the ability to plan ahead, communicate information properly, and assist others in developing both personally and professionally. Mentors assist mentees in developing their managerial and leadership skills.
- Recognition as a leader and subject-matter authority; improvement of their leadership techniques and guidance for businesses.

Numerous chances exist in your contact with a mentee to develop and practise interpersonal abilities, including communication, active listening, empathy, and patience. As you may meet frequently to discuss the mentee's objectives, thoughts, or problems as well as to give instructions or advice, communication is extremely important to mentoring.

- Beyond mentoring, having excellent interpersonal skills may facilitate connection building and enhance teamwork.
- Through mentoring, you may expand your network and even connect with someone who is completely different from you. You and your mentee may, for instance, come from different generations or backgrounds. You could change your attitude or learn something new by listening to your mentee's point of view. This skill can aid in developing more original or imaginative ideas at work.

Being of assistance may be fulfilling and important. Being seen as someone's source of wisdom is also a huge praise. In this partnership, there is mutual knowledge exchange. Mentors not only get insight into the issues and objectives of younger employees, but they may also receive a first-hand peek at cutting-edge tools or methods of operation.

- You impart pertinent knowledge acquired via your job or experience when working with a mentee. You provide them with advice or show them how to carry out particular responsibilities.
- You may instruct your mentee on negotiating techniques and then have them practise them with you. While the goal is to support the mentee's professional development, sharing this information helps you to solidify it internally. You may teach them techniques you no longer employ frequently, which would enable you to improve or rebuild those techniques.
- Mentorship may provide you with inner fulfilment in addition to granting you recognition or other exterior advantages. You may feel good knowing that you had a favourable influence on someone's life or career.

> *"According to the study, many professionals are actively seeking mentorship programmes to enhance their careers. Here are some of the benefits of mentoring programmes that help mentors and mentees advance in their careers."*

- Serving as a mentor might be a chance to mentor others if you were mentored early in your career. And one day, you could give their mentee the motivation they need to do the same for someone else.
- By discussing ideas and theories that the mentee will employ throughout his or her career, mentors gain first-

hand experience that helps them improve their own communication abilities. Thus, this information and idea exchange benefits both parties.

- If your mentee has considerable success, it will show others how valuable you are. Your leadership has contributed to some of their achievements, which can aid in your peers and coworkers recognising the abilities and expertise you have to give.

Other people can express an interest in working with you or request your mentoring. Along with giving you a sense of accomplishment, this admiration or favourable reputation could also open up more job chances for you.

- Through mentoring, you may reflect on and discuss your experiences. You could learn lessons from both your positive and negative experiences that help the mentee and yourself.
- Having a mentor may also help you remember why you love what you do, which will increase your level of engagement at work. You might also consider strategies to make the situation better if you find that you are dissatisfied with any aspect.
- Participating in a mentorship programme may significantly improve both your professional and personal interaction skills. As you go through the stages of your profession, you learn the art of inspiring and encouraging people to do better.
- It also demonstrates your abilities as a leader who can foster the development of others. By allowing you to exercise your persuading and motivating abilities on your mentors in a secure setting, mentoring programmes can help you get there faster.

Build on your strengths and get over your weaknesses; advice on career progress and development; increased awareness and exposure inside the organisation; exposure to new viewpoints, concepts, and techniques; improvement of one's career. As a mentor for those who are willing to devote their time to helping another professional, the connection delivers rewards that are mutual.

> *"A mentor is, to put it simply, a person with expertise in a certain area of managing a successful business. They are aware of the value of wisdom and experience. Growth and development are the main focus of the mentoring relationship between a mentor and an entrepreneur."*

Being a mentor has been really beneficial for me. My ability to connect with older and younger colleagues has improved as a result of my increased understanding of how they think and what is important in their lives. In addition, mentoring has improved my ability to listen and offer open-minded questions. It's been encouraging to see my mentees come up with creative solutions to issues that I never would have thought to address on my own. I occasionally found it difficult when my mentees brought up problems for which I had no idea. Working through the problem with the mentee made me realise that I don't necessarily need to know the solutions, but that by posing the correct queries, I may assist them in finding their own solutions.

Not everyone will get along with you. Personality problems can surface within the first two weeks, and other times they take much longer to manifest. No matter when the issue first arises, keep an eye on it. Speak with the mentorship program's coordinators. Change to a new mentee or mentor if you need to—just do it! I was reluctant to speak out when I encountered a comparable problem (in a different setting). Because of this, I implore everyone to speak up and take action—however challenging it may be.

Here are some pointers on how to improve your mentoring abilities:

"In order to close critical skill gaps, a smart mentor knows how to strengthen your shortcomings and enhance your strengths."

Being a mentor does not require you to grant every request, and I would advise against it. Don't take on too much; in this case, the proverb "quality over quantity" is applicable. Keep in mind that this relationship should be advantageous to both parties; don't accept it out of politeness; accept it because you have something to contribute.

"A mentor is a person who serves as a mentor to a mentee, a person with less expertise. Typically, people look for mentors in their sector or a related one. The mentor supports this person's professional growth and development by frequently providing guidance based on their more extensive knowledge or expertise. Building mentorship ties may be done through official mentorship programmes, networking, or personal connections."

The essential element in all relationships, still applies to this one. Any mentoring partnership that is not based on a foundation of mutual respect and trust will not be fruitful and will not last. Being an effective mentor has nothing to do with being haughty, showcasing one's expertise, or downplaying the mentee's lack of it.

- A mentor may share opportunities, introduce mentees to people who can advance their careers, and promote events and stretch assignments that will expose mentees to crucial knowledge and contacts.
- Mentors support and facilitate the growth of another person's career or personal life. Setting goals and providing feedback from a mentor might help them concentrate their efforts. As a result, businesses that desire to develop the talents of their employees frequently develop mentorship programmes.
- With the mentors' expertise, a skilled and effective staff may be developed. Employees like working environments that support professional growth because it shows that their employer cares about them and wants to see them succeed.

Essential Tips For Mentors:

- Clear limits from the beginning to prevent interpersonal conflicts, but give both you and your mentee time to adjust. There will be mistakes and misunderstandings. Discuss what would make the experience valuable for both of you and your mentee.
- Attend professional events together that are free. An excellent way to enhance your connection and satisfy your demand for professional growth at the same time is to choose and attend activities with your mentee. As an alternative, you may offer a few activities and ask your mentee which one seems most attractive.
- Respect the professional and personal history of your mentee. Whenever anything is confusing, get further

information. Don't leap to conclusions or render a hasty judgement.

- Limit the number of mentees you take on. Maintain mental clarity.
- Mentors can discuss ideas and suggestions for their mentees' future careers while they listen to their worries. Mentors may also provide comments and guidance that may assist a person to clearly see their next steps in a certain circumstance or with reference to their professional trajectory.

A mentor can assist people who are just starting their careers in establishing standards for what is expected of them professionally. For instance, they could make clear the importance of the position and acceptable workplace conduct. These recommendations may help the mentee establish beneficial working habits that will improve their focus and job completion.

> *"Mentoring is a two-way street where mentors should consider what their mentees can teach them. Find a mentor whose experiences or abilities you'd want to learn more about. For both parties, reverse mentoring may be a great benefit."*

Mentors should use strategie and other tried-and-true mentoring best practises. Every mentoring relationship should begin with a mentoring agreement that details the expectations, commitment, and aspirations of the mentee.

You must also prepare; you cannot wing this. You prepare similarly by having some questions ready. Keep in mind that you are attempting to determine how your mentee learns best and how they came to be in the situation they are in. Those two things alone will help you learn a little bit more about them.

It's likely that you don't know this individual very well, depending on how you two connected (via a programme or a common acquaintance), and the initial encounter will be dominated by the customary "get to know you questions."

- Have a few of these thoughtful questions prepared; they will help the conversation move along a lot more easily.
- Make it clear to mentees that it is their responsibility to lead the conversation and be prepared for each meeting. Mentees should also share updates and report on their progress towards goals.
- Meetings should be scheduled in advance, and an agenda should be sent so that the mentor has time to consider what suggestions or examples to make.

> "*According to me, because expectations are set forth in this initial agreement, clarity will lead to greater outcomes. Keeping in touch with one another will help your relationship succeed as you monitor your progress toward your goals and change your expectations as necessary.*"

- Encourage your mentee to utilise time carefully so that you may have time for conversation because this is a dialogue rather than a monologue.
- Mentors might also discuss the errors they made while travelling. The mentee gains from this since they are taught lessons about the detrimental effects of their mistakes without really having to experience them. Learning about these experiences may also help the

mentee get ready for the obstacles they will likely face and offer practical guidance on how to get through them.

- Mentors can provide their mentees with specialised knowledge and insights that help them succeed. They provide guidance on how to carry out certain activities or acquire practical skills, for instance. Such advice can be helpful to those who are just starting their careers since it enables them to become more at ease in their positions more rapidly. A mentor, for instance, can teach someone beginning a firm how to create their initial business plan and budget.

They may increase their productivity and wow their managers with these productive work practices. People should, if feasible, pick mentors who have the necessary experience for their career or aspirations. When mentors share their accomplishments, the mentee can use them as a benchmark and model the actions they performed.

As devoted to mentoring as you are to receiving it, a true mentor will always be. Similar to this, a successful mentoring relationship cannot be based on a one-way street between the mentor and the mentee. The unpleasant truth is that you cannot mentor someone who doesn't want to be a mentee, despite the fact that a mentor might be dedicated and offer great advise. Therefore, if you're not dedicated to the process, don't spend your or your mentee's time, and don't waste your own time on someone who doesn't respect your counsel.

- Mentors often do not ask for compensation because mentoring happens through networking or workplace initiatives. They volunteer to fill this function because they sincerely wish to support the other person's development and forge a more sincere and intimate relationship. Additionally, because mentoring is not paid for, it is available to all sorts of individuals rather than just those who can afford it.

- They may assist mentees with setting objectives and finding resources, as well as propose areas for professional growth that should be prioritised. Mentors may also be useful throughout the interview or promotion process, providing input on cover letters and resumes as well as advice on how to ace a meeting.
- Mentors should be explicit about what they intend to gain from exchanges and should steer dialogues and interactions. Set up the meeting times and settings and arrive prepared with questions, specific requests for help, and suggested conversation topics.

As a leader, your primary duty is to the organisation as a whole, and if you spend your mentoring time on futile projects, you are gating rather than stimulating growth. It makes sense to select people who share the same corporate goals and are motivated to advance their personal abilities for the good of the business. While not everyone is born with the same amount of self-assurance or attributes needed to serve as a mentor, anyone may acquire these abilities and do so.

- As soon as a new employee completes the responsibilities allocated to them, let them know you would be happy to assist them. Then, be accessible if they so request it. If one has never completed a time sheet before, it may seem impossible. Don't hold off until someone asks.

- It's difficult to provide frank criticism. It necessitates extraordinary communication abilities and a degree of transparency that few people find comfortable.
- When you introduce your informal mentees, inform them of their positions within the company. Being able to network is a crucial talent for each employee to have, because we cannot successfully do our duties on our own. The mentee will be ready to take someone with them eventually through growing their network.
- Analysing a person's work path may be enlightening. Mentors provide information on a broad and local scale, including the specifics of job triumphs (how to build a successful, fulfilling career).
- As a supporter of a mentee's ambitions and desires, mentors may also provide encouragement.

> *"Clear, attainable objectives that both the mentor and the mentee may strive toward are necessary for successful mentoring programmes. These objectives will promote a sense of progress and purpose."*

The ability to control expectations in terms of communication is essential for success. Both the mentee and the mentor must understand the scope of the connection and the frequency of communication necessary each month. This early agreement ensures that commitments are kept and boundaries are understood.

Effective partnerships take a variety of things into account when matching applicants. The proposed mentors and mentees should be matched based on shared goals, experiences, and personalities. This will guarantee that the right matches are made and fruitful connections are created.

"Encourage, equip, empower, energise, and elevate while engaging others. These are the techniques for optimising any person's, group's, institution's, or organisation's potential for success and importance in the long run. The techniques of a mentor leader are those."

When people link their jobs with their deeper human motivations and beliefs, it benefits both employers and workers. Mentorship helps people do this. Despite increased efforts by businesses, Gallup reports that roughly 85% of employees throughout the world are still neither engaged nor actively disengaged at work.

The characteristics of and perspectives on leadership are evolving on a global scale. Let's begin by defining a leader in order to see whether they vary. A leader is someone who directs and leads an individual or group of individuals toward a certain goal. A manager hired by a business owner is an example of a well-defined leadership job.

Leadership can also be assumed based on an individual's personal traits. Who then serves as a mentor? He is someone who also leads someone else or a group of people in the direction of a goal, but often on a voluntary basis rather than under the auspices of a formal arrangement.

Many people consider mentoring to be primarily a moral responsibility. But what's frequently overlooked is the fact that mentoring is a kind of self-improvement. Better leadership can result from this kind of development, giving both the mentor and the mentee "career currency" from the exchange.

Many organisations use training courses that concentrate on developing leadership abilities with a particular emphasis on mentoring. A mentoring relationship may be a rewarding experience that aids in the development of your communication and leadership abilities as well as your own professional growth. Knowing that you're assisting someone else in their career and personal growth through mentoring may also make you feel really satisfied overall.

In my opinion, this is something that all of us who serve as leaders must be accountable for. You must consider the individual's talents, temperament, passions, accomplishments, joys, and opportunities. Once you've located that seed, you need to water it with opportunity and nourish it with encouragement. If you do, you'll see the individual grow before your very eyes.

It is crucial that company leaders choose the best sort of mentoring to ensure that the connection and outcomes are extremely beneficial. Here are some common mentorship roles to think about pursuing:

Business leaders must evaluate the career aspirations of their mentees and work to match them with the objectives of the company. Young professionals who want to advance in their careers might benefit greatly from receiving career development advice. Additionally, it fosters the growth of new talents and a sense of community among younger employees. Once high potentials (HiPos) have been identified, firms must invest differently in them since they will eventually be the organisation's leaders. Business coaches must be focused.

Trust and support are the cornerstones of great mentoring. Additionally, the company leader must consistently build and maintain the mentoring connection. As a confidant and counsellor to the mentee, the mentor serves as a source of advice. Ideally, the connection will develop over time.

Regardless of whether your company has a structured mentorship programme or not, we should be considering how we may bring someone along with us. Informally, mentoring is when one individual receives guidance from another. The word "chooses" makes a difference in this case. Every seasoned individual should consider this since it may lead to a relationship that is advantageous to both the mentor and the mentee. Consider someone you can mentor today, and consider how you can implement one or more of the suggestions below to help a coworker.

How organisational leadership are going to get benefited by mentorship programme?

For organisation, engaging in mentoring is a realistic and economical way to develop qualified young talent and maintain the interest and motivation of their knowledgeable and more seasoned employees. Fostering a culture of both professional and personal development; cultivate a climate of personal and professional development; encourage professional conduct and attitudes inside the organisation boost managers' coaching and leadership abilities; attract, hold on to, and nurture colleagues.

There are instances when mentoring benefits employee engagement initiatives:

- By utilising the experience of your more senior staff, it expands the opportunities for training and growth.
- Mentorship helps workers communicate with management, removing communication obstacles.
- By putting what they discuss in their mentoring meetings into reality, both mentors and mentees get the chance to demonstrate their abilities.

- Relationships at work have a strong impact on engagement. Mentorship fosters the social connections that prevent workers from losing hope and promotes a development mentality.
- Mentoring holds mentors and mentees accountable for the obligations they make to one another.It is more difficult to put off doing what needs to be done to develop when you make a commitment to grow with a mentor.

Because it provides great achievers with personal and professional growth, mentoring raises employee engagement. It satisfies their need for professional advancement as well as the expansion of their knowledge and skill sets.

- The benefits of mentoring include the opportunity to give back and the fact that mentoring is a crucial learning and development process. The best way to learn is to teach others. Likewise, when they mentor and support young talent, mentors develop their skills as communicators and leaders.
- Giving mentors the opportunity to serve as role models can improve their leadership skills and boost their confidence. The senior employee must mentor, inspire, and provide candid criticism in challenging conversations in order to assist someone to achieve their career and aspirations. These abilities are at the top of the list of prerequisites for a leader.
- Mentors will get recognition for their communication abilities and capacity to assist young workers with their career growth and personal development, much like how leaders build their leadership skills. Mentors will

come to be recognised as open-minded counsellors.

Albert Einstein famously stated, "If you can't explain it to a six-year-old, you don't comprehend it yourself." Similar to this, if you've ever had to explain something to someone, you'll undoubtedly have realised that you had to consider it carefully and simplify your explanation in order to make it understandable for someone else. Due to their involvement in mentoring relationships, mentors will improve their listening and communication skills.

- A mentoring relationship can assist the more seasoned employee in picking up new skills, even if the mentor is often in the position of teaching the mentee new information. By using a reverse mentoring strategy, younger workers frequently assume the position of mentor to discuss technical advancements, trends, or hone their digital abilities. In this area, the mentee can also act as a mentor, helping the mentor pick up new abilities or methods of operation.
- By assisting in the training of new and emerging workers, the mentor has the chance to give back to the organisation while also enhancing the competence and satisfaction of those around them. It's a fantastic chance to identify emerging talent for advancements or unique initiatives. The networks of both the mentor and mentee benefit from mentoring.
- Because you work closely with someone to support their professional development, mentoring is a leadership job. They should learn important talents or progress in their careers through your guidance. This experience demonstrates your leadership abilities, which are important for any career or function. It also shows how

well you can direct others toward a common objective. This experience can help you progress professionally.

Participating in mentorship programmes can demonstrate your value for building relationships and advancing others' careers. Your mentee receives guidance and instruction from you, but you also gain knowledge from them. They can teach you about topics you have never encountered before if you and your mentee have diverse backgrounds. The mentee may have knowledge of the most recent trends or procedures, even though you have greater industry experience. If your mentee is younger and more technologically savvy, they might be able to teach you how to use new software, for instance.

No matter what stage of your career you are in, adding a mentorship experience will help you stand out from the competition. Your ability to apply your knowledge to help others is illustrated by this encounter. You may boost your confidence by supporting your mentee's success. It proves that you possess traits that encourage the growth or development of others. You may increase your career and personal self-worth by having this confidence. You might feel more secure in your abilities and the regular work you generate if you have that confidence. When bargaining with managers for promotions, increases, or other possibilities for growth, this confidence is essential.

In addition to good commercial results, these abilities can create a pleasant culture and more productive teamwork in addition to good commercial results. By taking part in an employer's mentoring programme, you may assist in developing their workers by using your expertise. These workers may become more effective and productive if they comprehend the demands of their jobs and develop good work habits.

More than 90% of mentors said that the experience improved them as leaders or managers at work. In fact, establishing interpersonal skills that foster purpose or rapport is directly applicable to fundamental ideas like situational leadership, where an accurate evaluation of an employee's requirements and those of a particular scenario helps everyone succeed. We encourage leaders who believe that mentoring is one more item they should be focusing on right now to consider mentoring as a liberating tool that will enable your team to help one another. We also hope you will find meaning in mentoring.

I refer to a mentoring relationship that provides something profound to both the mentee and the mentor as transformational mentoring, and it takes equal effort from both parties. The key to properly engaging your mentor as a mentee is to choose the appropriate person—someone with whom you can develop a casual, motivating friendship that is motivated by curiosity rather than the binary instructor-student interaction we typically teach.

Essential Tips For Organisational Leadership

As long as there is a shared desire for personal and professional advancement, these mentorships can be developed with those who are more senior to you or peers of similar standing. Take Albert Einstein's interactions with Werner Heisenberg and Niels Bohr as one of the best instances. They had different backgrounds and ages, but they were all fascinated by theoretical physics. In a period of rapid technological change and invention, each of them was able to make significant strides in their respective fields because of their open dialogue and sincere interest. The three physicists communicated and met over a long period of time. They weren't competing with one another;

they didn't frequently dispute or advocate a certain viewpoint. Instead, they shared opinions, made queries, provided insights, and encouraged one another's outlandish ideas.

A potential mentor could appear ideal on paper, but if you actually meet them, they might not be a good match (whether virtually or in-person). In order for the relationship to flourish, you need to establish a sincere connection. Therefore, start small.

Decide whether you can meet them for lunch or coffee. Do your research in advance by investigating particular subjects that could be of interest to you. Check out their podcast interviews, presentations, social media feeds, and written pieces that have been published. Remember that this initial conversation doesn't have to be big. Whatever you discuss, look for ways to provide value by contemplating how you will express your own connected interests and insights or by coming up with fascinating articles you may share on the subject.

Don't strive to impress your possible mentor throughout the chat; instead, let their interests guide you. Through your inquiries, you may demonstrate your authority and interest in their job. Pay attention to their degree of participation and the questions they ask you in return to decide whether the conversation is mutually beneficial.

Try to gradually shift the conversation to topics relevant to your career: What impact may digitalisation have on the world's supply chains? Will escalating international conflict affect world trade? How should we assess the output of knowledge workers and how do they wish to be managed? Pay close attention to their replies, perspectives, and opinions. Do you find them inspiring? If true, it may be a match.

Employers continue to witness large numbers of their best employees leaving in search of brighter pastures. 40% of respondents to Microsoft's Work Trend Index 2021 study of more than 30,000 workers in 31 countries said they planned to hunt for new employment.

"A McKinsey survey found that 41% of those who quit do so for lack of job advancement. An increasing number of professionals are reassessing their objectives and determining what they want and desire from their companies."

Lani Phillips, a Microsoft executive, asserts that organisations have underestimated mentoring as a talent management strategy. According to her, when done correctly, it may drastically alter a worker's involvement with their employer. The data supports this.

According to a 2019 poll, 91% of workers who have a mentor are content at work. This is significant since just 20% of employees worldwide, according to Gallup, are truly engaged in their work. According to a different study, people who have mentors tend to retain information 50% better than those who don't. In the present competition for talent, no firm can develop without keeping people engaged, and mentoring is a proven method of employee retention.

One of the obstacles to a strong mentoring relationship is that too many leaders claim they don't have time to devote to mentoring. The reality is that mentoring is our duty as a leader to encourage and train those who want to succeed and develop their careers. Time is undoubtedly a valuable resource, but mentoring should be viewed as an expense rather than a cost. And when you consider the expenses associated with finding and developing new people, this investment makes sense.

When assessing mentoring relationships, include the required time to get it right, such as preparing and supporting the mentee. Make it a priority at work and include it in your monthly or quarterly routine. As you establish a reputation for talent development and update your organisation's leadership techniques, your personal brand will rise.

The classic mentoring paradigm is a series of one-on-one encounters. This methodology hasn't changed to accommodate employees' current needs or make use of all the potent coaching tools available. Leaders can distribute fictitious homework, exercises, books, podcasts, movies, TED speeches, and articles with insightful career guidance. These digital tools are part of a developing trend that I call "digital mentoring."

Mentees should be aware that learning may come from a number of sources, and a good mentor will encourage them to regularly seek out opportunities for learning and inspiration. Despite the fact that many professionals enter the corporate world with protective armour in the shape of bachelor's degrees , they are insufficient to ward off the whims of the competitive environment. The consoling and directing assistance of a leader who has, as they say, "been there, done that" therefore acquires crucial significance.

This is not entirely unexpected. After all, it is impossible to overstate the value of a guide. This is not to imply that having a mentor by your side will guarantee that the sun will shine brilliantly, a trail of flowers will materialise before the budding professional, and that lulling music will play in the background as you watch them win after win. By every measure, the business climate is unpredictable. The ever-changing course that enterprises must take on a daily basis is determined by both internal and external variables.

"Many top organisations have established "Management Training Programs" or an equivalent for young professionals in order to familiarise them with the many aspects of work and start them out on the proper foot."

Some of the more progressive ones established a "mentor-mentee" programme, which lasts longer than the original hiring stage and serves as a formative role for mid-level managers, with the aim of enhancing their competencies and preparing them for more senior responsibilities. Beyond this is the mentoring connection that naturally develops between a senior leader (often a supervisor) and a professional because the two get along and feel comfortable after working together for a while.

We have seen the terminology of the development plan grow to represent a much larger view of human development as organisations change in the digital era. When viewed in the context of the shifting workplace ecosystem of today, a straightforward 5-point plan that links the organisational charter to training plans appears shortsighted. A development plan is all about carefully cultivating your human wealth with purpose and compassion. Traditionally, development plans have only been used to upskill personnel to meet the future demands of a company and industry.

Emotional intelligence, cultural sensitivity, strategic intent, physical health, financial savvy, etc. all form a part of holistic human development and are blended into the plans, structured or otherwise. This is in addition to skill upgrades as required by the business.

A people manager's job must change from that of a supervisor to that of a coach or mentor for such an approach to succeed. A development plan constructed in this manner would also transfer responsibility for personal growth from the boss to the individual. The primary concept is to establish an atmosphere that is conducive to identifying growth requirements, both those linked to core functional areas and those connected to personal traits, rather than for the organisation to prescribe one's development goals.

Modifying ingrained human behaviour will undoubtedly require consistent effort. However challenging an employee's behaviour may seem, when thoroughly examined, it is actually personal experiences, a lack of exposure to the situation, the correct knowledge at the right moment, or both that determine employee behaviour. Perhaps no one has ever made an effort to get to know a reclusive employee or asked them to come out of their shell. They most likely want to change but aren't sure what to do next.

The tech industry alone has enormous development potential, especially given the abundance of employment centred around new technologies. It will be fascinating to see if the workforce is prepared physically, cognitively, financially, and emotionally to handle the demands of the digital revolution even though it is ready to take on these new jobs head-on.

Are we, as people leaders, asking ourselves this question before putting up development plans and matching them to organisational requirements?

If we were to rate ourselves as employers who empower workers holistically to be more effective in their jobs, what would our organisational scorecard look like?

However, the capacity of the manager to demonstrate to staff members the bigger picture and how their behaviour is related to their career trajectory is crucial to developing emotional intelligence (EI). An employee's long-term professional goals may be hazy, but you may help them by providing mentoring so they can see things more clearly. Finally, take your time when researching. Set a high standard. This is a relationship, not simply a mentorship, and it has the potential to alter the direction of your career.

"When you do come across someone who embodies these qualities and who motivates you, focus on building a connection with them rather than approaching them about being your mentor straight away. Over time, you won't feel pressured to ask them to serve as your mentor; instead, you'll just be receiving advice from a friend. The optimal cadence will be determined by you and your mentor at the end."

- Dr. Amit Das

CHAPTER THREE

Implementation Of Mentorship In Your Organisation

"I've learned that people will forget what you said, people will forget what you did, but people will never forget how you made them feel." — Maya Angelou

The success of the employee and the organisation depend on developing the appropriate knowledge, skills, and expertise at the appropriate time.

We are aware that employees with a sense of belonging make greater contributions to the company and stick around longer than those who don't. Yet far too many companies fail to see how crucial it is to both their retention of current talent and business success. Even if businesses are able to retain their workers, a lack of a sense of belonging will lower engagement, creating a staff that is unmotivated and unproductive and negatively affecting their employer brand. According to my research, 43% of office workers think that having a sense of value is more essential than receiving financial rewards like bonus plans and health insurance. This shows a noticeable change in how workers see the place of work in their lives.

> *"According to the most recent study, 16 million office workers do not currently feel as though they belong in their current organisation, and 72% of these people want to leave their jobs in the upcoming year. This indicates that 11.5 million people will consider leaving their jobs in 2022."*

Mentoring can aid in increasing retention and reducing turnover. According to Deloitte, 68% of millennials who have a mentor plan to work for the company for five years (compared to 32% of millennials who do not have a mentor). 82% of respondents to the moving ahead research who feel mentoring relationships assist in establishing meaningful connections between mentors and mentees across departments and the organisation said they believe this increases employee engagement.

> *"Mentoring may help integrate individuals into company culture and make them feel that the firm cares about them."*

Mentorship is important in developing critical knowledge and skills. We frequently hear trainees from different companies use the phrases "mentorship" and "leadership" interchangeably when we communicate with them. It's interesting that practically everyone who is asked what they want from their elders says they want a mentor, not a leader. With millennials entering the workforce and their desire to not just follow, this is growing in popularity.

Why should organisations use mentoring as a competitive tool?

Companies profit from a highly trained workforce but also from the desire of employees to advance in their careers. By modelling characteristics, abilities, and behaviours that the person being mentored can imitate, a mentor serves as a role model for that individual. When we examine any successful organisation, we find that they cultivate a culture in which the development, application, and transfer of knowledge and skills are highly valued, suggesting that leaders must embrace mentoring for the overall success of their organisations.

By modelling qualities, abilities, and behaviours that the person being mentored can imitate, a mentor serves as a role model for the other person. The power that a person has over her followers is the key distinction between leaders and mentors. A leader has a well-established power over his followers, whereas mentors typically use a more liberal strategy by offering advice and letting the other person decide whether to put it into effect or not. Sincerity be damned, I believe that mentoring and leadership go hand in hand. In actuality, a person can only be considered a real leader if he or she is an effective mentor. When I examine any successful organisations, I find that they cultivate a culture in which the development, application, and transfer of knowledge and skills are highly valued, suggesting that leaders must embrace mentoring for the overall success of their organisations.

Many aspiring professionals ignore the value of developing their professional networks, which always comes in useful in the corporate world. Your mentor may assist you in doing this. When a mentoring relationship is successful, it can increase the mentee's drive and involvement. It's fantastic news for your organisation's future leadership pipeline, whether you already have a mentorship programme or unofficial mentoring ties between employees and supervisors. However, you might want to give that a go if you haven't already. However, keep in mind that while preserving the current reporting connections, both employees and managers are eager to participate in this relationship with the added obligations of communication.

How can mentoring programmes be used to improve employee performance and reduce attrition?

There are multiple ways that formal mentor programmes benefit businesses. Companies that invest the time and resources or support initiatives for mentorship programmes may generate a beneficial influence on their recruitment efforts, general corporate culture, and employee engagement and therefore become a wonderful place to work. Mentorship programmes as an idea aren't really a new idea. This procedure has become very common because, in the past, experienced employees served as "buddy" to new hires, teaching them the ropes and introducing them to the company. However, the growth of formal mentor programmes in the current, fiercely competitive, global economy shows how businesses feel they may contribute to revenue growth and save costs.

A low-cost strategy to raise employee engagement in your workforce is to implement mentoring programmes. These initiatives support the professional growth of your staff members and foster a coaching culture that boosts output. For instance, Time Warner Cable believes that through increasing staff loyalty and retention, their mentorship programme promotes employee happiness.

They take pride in having a culture where mentors educate new hires on the specifics of the position and so play a crucial role in developing future leaders. Because of the emergence of a multigenerational workforce, mentoring is not only intended for junior management staff.

All generations of employees are now learning from one another. Companies are increasingly promoting sessions for various classes of coworkers to exchange their expertise and skills as the reverse mentoring phenomenon has gained recognition. According to the Wall Street Journal, businesses including Hewlett-Packard, Cisco, and Ogilvy & Mather have already seen success after implementing official reverse mentorship programmes. increases retention and hiring.

Similar like mentees, mentors benefit from the process of mentoring their mentees by expanding their knowledge and developing deeper insights into their areas of interest. This fosters a culture of learning and sharing inside the company, which is advantageous to everyone working there. Mentorship programmes may have a favourable effect on a company's recruiting efforts, general corporate culture, and employee engagement. Mentoring programmes may have a good effect on a company's recruiting efforts, general corporate culture, and employee engagement, making it a fantastic place to work. Companies who invest the time and resources or support initiatives for mentorship programmes can do this.

Business mentors should concentrate on introducing HiPos to various business sectors, fostering their leadership potential, and offering them novel and interesting employment options. Business executives, HR, and L&D all share responsibilities for mentoring. It is a never-ending journey with a connection that is always developing and yielding greater advantages for both people and the company. Senior corporate leaders have the chance to make a lasting impression by guiding talent down the correct path through mentoring. Furthermore, it creates new opportunities for young people to advance in their careers.

"There isn't just one right approach to mentoring someone. Depending on the mentor-mentee connection or the approach used, we may categorise different mentoring strategies."

The ability to recruit and sustain transformational mentor connections depends on that spirit. Employees desire the chance to develop and learn, especially in light of the Great Resignation. In fact, more than 66% of workers are ready to retrain and upgrade their skills for new positions. The urge to take online classes alone is decreasing, though. Many people would rather receive one-on-one or group mentorship instead of merely taking online courses alone.

How have people's perceptions of receiving or providing mentoring altered as a result of hybrid remote work?

Individualised Mentoring

One-on-one coaching is the most common and intimate kind of mentoring. It simply includes the mentor and the mentee. In this mentorship, a more-experienced professional is matched with a less-experienced or younger mentee.

Groups Mentoring :

One or more mentors work with a group of mentees in this kind of mentoring approach. These mentorship programmes are often formal in nature at work. A group of mentees is often trained by a mentor on work procedures and other relevant topics. A more extensive version of one-on-one mentoring is group mentoring. Due to a shortage of time or resources, the mentors here work with bigger groups. It is a successful strategy for upskilling organisations.

Peer Mentoring:

Participants in peer mentoring are from the same department or job. On the basis of his expertise and experience, the mentor leads the mentee. Peer mentoring relationships can be one-on-one or in a group setting.

E-Mentoring:

The mentorship method has altered during the last few years. It is not restricted to in-person contact. Organizations are starting to use e-mentorship models, which allow mentors and mentees to communicate online at predetermined times.

Reverse mentoring:

This one is intriguing. In such a mentor-mentee relationship, a younger or junior professional instructs the senior members on how to work on a new technology or application. Filling in the skill gaps has been shown to be a successful use of reverse mentoring. It also teaches how to adjust to possibilities for quick learning.

Spot Mentoring:

This kind of mentoring is concentrated on brief, one-time meetings to master a crucial skill or piece of information. Flash mentoring is currently a well-liked method of meeting new mentors and mentees and encourages business networking with the top executives.

Transformational mentoring:

These are especially well suited for innovators in other disciplines. When you share ideas with one another, you could each learn new perspectives that you hadn't previously considered. This will encourage you both to think outside the box and put yourself in a better position to profit from emerging trends in your respective industries. Leverage your professional network to identify these individuals, but push yourself to connect with completely unfamiliar contacts rather than the most well-known people on LinkedIn.

> *"Research demonstrates that organisations that set up formal mentoring programmes create a strong and engaged work culture, with employees more likely to learn and advance inside the company rather than leave."*

In order to recruit and keep top talent and produce fresh ideas that will lead to corporate success, it is realistic to expect that firms will spend more money in the future on developing successful mentorship programmes. One of the key things I look for in a candidate's curriculum vitae when we interview candidates for openings at our company is articles and presentations. I am more interested in the number of authors than the quantity of papers or journals in which their work appeared or the names of their presentations. More precisely, did they work alone or in collaboration with other employees? This tells me a lot about whether the person is working with others or working on their own.

What do mentoring programs aim to achieve?

The goal of mentoring is to develop by drawing on the wisdom and experience of someone who has gone before you. The best approach to quickening your growth is to do it. In this manual, we cover every aspect of mentoring, including its advantages, characteristics of effective mentors, applications in the workplace, and how to start a mentorship program. The goal of mentoring is to pair up someone with extensive knowledge and experience with someone who hasn't yet attained the same levels of expertise.

You can get knowledge from experiences other than your own by asking someone with more experience than you for advice, direction, and to act as a sounding board for your ideas. Having a mentor is essential to your continuing development in both your work and life.

Employee retention is one of the most important concerns for businesses in 2022. Many employees had to reconsider the importance of employment in their lives as a result of the global epidemic. The outcome? The great resignation organisations nowadays are looking for whatever strategy they can find to lower employee turnover. Many people are beginning to focus on mentorship. That raises the question of whether mentoring is a practical strategy for retaining and energising employees.

Do you require assistance utilising mentoring data to support mentoring at your company?

Effective, high-quality data is increasingly essential to every sector, but talent management in particular. Business executives rely on solid data for every decision they make, including ongoing cost/benefit analysis of current engagement methods or investigations into the potential ROI of developing new ones. This involves deciding whether to start or grow mentorship programmes. Research data stating that 70% of Fortune 500 businesses implemented mentorship programmes in 2019-20.

According to a new, comprehensive research of the mentoring environment across US Fortune 500 companies, it is time to retire this often referenced data point in favour of the following salient conclusions, according to a new, comprehensive research of the mentoring environment across US Fortune 500 companies:

- Mentoring programmes are available at 84% of Fortune 500 companies in the United States.
- All 50 Fortune 500 firms in the US provide mentorship programmes.
- During the 2020-Covid-19 economic crisis, US Fortune 500 firms with mentorship programmes on average saw higher profitability.
- Following the 2020 COVID-19 economic crisis, firms with female CEOs saw the least impact on their profitability.
- Despite having notoriously high staff turnover rates, firms in the retail, automotive, and food and beverage industries make up the majority of those on the US Fortune 500 list without mentorship programmes.

What drives demand for mentoring?

Mentorship is becoming a need rather than a luxury. It is crucial for companies that wish to flourish in the post-pandemic environment. If the "Great Resignation" has taught us everything, it is that employees with in-demand skills are willing to leave their current employer in search of one that provides a better quality of life, better work-life balance, higher pay, more opportunities for upskilling and reskilling, and opportunities for deeper and more meaningful workplace connections and interactions.

The UK registered 2.7 million job openings in 2022, making the competition for talent more severe than ever. As a result, worker retention is becoming more and more crucial. UK businesses simply cannot afford to lose brilliant employees because doing so now takes more time and money than ever. Given these figures, it is obvious that the value of belonging at work will continue to rise.

How can companies foster a welcoming environment and a community where everyone feels included?

There are strategies that may be used, such as mentorship programmes and digital platforms, that have been shown to be valued by employees and will assist companies in fostering a stronger feeling of belonging and community among their team.

Both the mentor and the mentee must put in time and effort. It takes work to succeed in your career. The corporate environment's ambiguity and unpredictability are, on the one hand, while employees' varied goals are, on the other. In this fast-paced environment, it's critical that employees receive the necessary motivation to advance their careers.

Because it can be used widely, digital mentoring is especially useful in fostering a sense of inclusion among all team members. It is also a useful tool for remote employees who cannot take advantage of the organic relationships developed in an office setting. My research reveals that nearly half of the employees who were able to maintain a feeling of community while working remotely during the epidemic attributed it to online support groups and mentorship programmes.

Learners may improve their skills and knowledge in a range of areas and have the flexibility to investigate issues with the greatest urgency and relevance since mentors can address whatever the learning demands are at the time without having to focus on a specified curriculum. Like investing, picking mentees is comparable. You hope for favourable results because you have fewer resources.

Being a mentor is a huge duty that may positively and significantly affect the career of a young professional. Good mentors take this responsibility seriously and put in the necessary effort to ensure that the mentee gets the most out of the relationship.

Do gender biases still exist in mentorship?

It says that when a male mentors a woman, the relationship is frequently strained by traditional gender norms and perhaps negative exterior judgments. Traditional ideas of mentorship are frequently based on relationships between males, the kinds that start on the golf course, are almost exclusively focused on professional success, and entail more than a few pats on the back over drinks after work. However, women frequently express a need for mentorship that balances their interpersonal and professional demands.

Women want a mentor who actually values this rather than just "getting" it. Men need to completely understand how important it is to encourage talented junior women in order for them to continue, advance, and succeed in their careers and organisations. A workplace's culture will grow more equal, productive, and likely to keep top talent as more women thrive, lean in, and take on leadership responsibilities.

However, the mentoring environment is uneven. Women regularly encounter greater obstacles than men in obtaining mentorships, and when they do, they may only experience a more limited set of career and psychological advantages.

A mentor advises her mentees to seek out coaching and therapy. Namita, a top executive at a manufacturer, has recently advanced one level at work. She prides herself on moving up the corporate ladder despite working in a field where men predominate.

She also chooses to mentor younger women at her company since she finds the gender gap quite upsetting. She decides to mentor no more than three mentees at a time due to time restrictions. When she has chosen all of her mentees, she eagerly begins the mentoring relationship with them, trying her best to inspire and assist these ladies in their professional endeavours. Namita learns from her mentees that two of them might gain from working with a coach or a counsellor as well, after a few chats with them.

For instance, Sheela , one of her mentees, is finding it difficult to deal with the unexpected death of her husband in a vehicle accident. Namita advises sheela to consult a bereavement counsellor for more help. Rhea, another of her mentees, is searching for strategies to improve work-life balance while still being a working mother. Namita advises Rhea to engage with a qualified coach who can spend more time ensuring that Rhea can make the adjustments in her life that are actually necessary for her wellbeing.

Namita is able to have a beneficial influence on her mentees' lives on many different levels by recognising when to provide her own experiences and advice and when to send her mentees to other experts. Minorities face challenges that wealthier workers do not. A mentorship programme may make it easier to spot emerging problems. It is about giving a diverse variety of workers the freedom to exchange thoughts, suggestions, information, and experiences on an even playing field. Mentors must focus on creating cultural awareness and cultivating trust and support.

Does your mentor have the necessary experience?

- A good mentor is aware of their limitations, particularly when it comes to matters of inclusion, equity, and diversity. If you're looking for a mentor to help you with a DEI issue, be careful to state that up front and create a situation where the potential mentor can say no. Although they can find resources to help you with your problem or link you with another good choice, they are unable to serve as your mentor.
- Mentors assist with implementation; mentees decide the agenda. Your responsibility as a mentee is to set the framework for your goals. Do you want coaching to help you start moving up to executive positions? Do you want to learn how to lead a team for the first time?
- A mentor helps employees feel appreciated and instils the organisation's ideals in them. The capacity of the manager to show employees the bigger picture and how their behaviour is related to their career trajectory is crucial to helping them develop emotional intelligence (EI).
- When your mentor is a leader inside your own organisation, it might be difficult to sidestep the conventional mentor- mentee model of mentoring. The disparity in your degrees of seniority is primarily to blame for this. Instead, consider exploring prospective mentors in environments unrelated to your line of work or your areas of interest.
- Consider your interests, hobbies, and curiosity as a starting point. Perhaps you are a content producer who has always been curious about cutting-edge technological advancements. There is a professional in this industry whose work you especially respect or whose social media updates provide you with inspiration.

- Even if their work seems unrelated to your own, don't pass them by. People that pique your interest are those whose experiences, wisdom, and actions may serve as a road map for all the directions your career may go.
- Do not confine yourself to a single person, always. Like with Einstein, sometimes the process functions best when there are several peers involved. Even if they don't work well together, you could discover value in each mentor individually at various points along your growth path.

Diverse culture All of the following questions should be answered with a loud "yes" if you, your team, and the organisation are all working together toward the same objective.

Does your company appreciate and include everyone in achieving its greater goals?

Workplace wellness is all the rage right now, and for good reason. Since most of their waking hours are spent at work, employees have very little time to adopt a schedule that prioritises their physical and mental health. Employees' potential for professional growth can only be realised when they are in good physical and mental health. The workplace gym is not the only facility that boosts employee enthusiasm. Regular wellness seminars, 24-hour access to counsellors for workers who need help managing pressure at work or outside of it, routine health check-ups, or just breaking up the monotony of work with occasional floor parties, are all important components of a well-rounded wellness program.

Is the long-term objective of your company well accepted across the board?

Is your team at your side as you define the organisation's growth path, providing you with actionable things for the near term and planning and a long-term vision? Financial well-being: It is generally recognised that worrying about money has a negative impact on productivity. Therefore, it is crucial to have a programme in place that informs staff of all available alternatives for creating a good financial plan. For individuals who support their families solely, this is more crucial. Personal money is and will be a touchy issue, but workers should be assured that support is available for those who require it with savings and investing.

Adopting such a strategy for personal development is undoubtedly impossible without the assistance of technology. The numerous applications and tools that are already on the market assist in creating and enacting holistic development plans, starting with the identification of the whole value and potential of humans and continuing all the way to realising it using self-paced, realistic ways. The layout of the strategy is more important than the programmes and technologies one utilises. A holistic strategy is required for this, in addition to making sufficient use of digital technologies. For organisations across all industries, having such a development strategy and a culture that supports it will be a strategic advantage.

Is reverse mentoring a possibility or a requirement?

Learning will pass between "older" workers and "younger" workers as well as vice versa. This will also be a crucial habit for maintaining the bonds between "generations" in order to achieve greater organisational goals. The effort known as "Reverse Mentoring," which lets leaders take on the role of mentees and access Gen Y ideas, is one of the enablers that will help this phenomenon take off.

"By 2024, millennials will make up about half of the workforce worldwide. With 64% of its population in the working age group, India will surpass Japan as the youngest nation in the world."

To stay current and in the know, businesses would undoubtedly prefer to tap into this group of workers. Younger workers are mentoring older and more senior executives and team members in a variety of areas, including technology, working methods, contemporary trends and lifestyles, and social media.

Reverse mentoring is a two-way relationship. Senior executives can gain knowledge from younger people. Trust and support are the cornerstones of great mentoring. Additionally, the company leader must consistently build and maintain the mentoring connection. As a confidant and counsellor to the mentee, the mentor serves as a source of advice.

"Reverse mentorship offers that chance, and mentors must be willing to learn from less-experienced employees."

Ideally, the connection will develop over time. Mentors must simultaneously watch the business environment for possibilities and risks that might affect their mentees, the department, and the organisation as a whole. Above all, mentors should serve as positive role models for mentees by upholding the ideals that are advantageous to the company. For this, they must be able to encourage, inspire, and assist younger workers in making the connection between their own objectives and beliefs and the wider organisational principles.

> *"Reverse mentoring is still a two-way process where both the mentor and the mentee may use the connection to further both their personal and professional development over time."*

Life expectancy at work is increasing. The number of generational overlaps may increase as work-life expectancy rises and we discover that we are still working at 75. By 2023, there may be five different generations (commonly referred to as generational "cohorts") working together. More distant futures are now in our sights: 10, 20, 50, and 65 years from now. There may be seven generations working simultaneously and colliding with one another.

The difficulty for businesses in the future will be incorporating these generations into the workforce. The fact that this variety will bring in a wide range of skill sets that can complement one another is, nevertheless, one of the positive elements. Businesses will be driven by a complex web of simple and complicated skill sets, so it will be crucial to employ a wide range of skill-sets and mindsets.

> *"In reverse mentoring, a younger individual may feel frightened by a leader's success and experience. The leaders are in charge of culturally integrating people from various age groups. Setting the stage for inclusion and respect involves recognising the skills, knowledge, and experience for which a person has been employed."*

As a result, people would need to undergo a significant mental transformation in order to understand that skill sets may need to be managed across generations and that one generation may not have all of the necessary abilities required to lead a business.

Therefore, when starting such projects, organisations should educate both the mentor and the mentee, match the pairs according to requirements and personalities, hold an introduction session to define expectations, and keep the door open for feedback.

There is a greater possibility that when we hear the phrase "mentor," we think of an elderly individual. But does a mentor always have to be an older person? Young professionals who are leaders in emerging fields of study or who are technological gurus have disproved this preconception. Many businesses pair a senior executive with a more junior executive to help with technological efforts. Reverse mentorship is being aggressively promoted by companies including GE, PepsiCo, Apple, IBM, Vodafone, Godrej, Jubilant Foods, and Forbes Marshall.

Another example is a huge technology corporation that runs a successful reverse mentoring programme for over 1,000 workers. In order for organisations to thrive in today's dynamic and technologically driven world, it is now crucial to combine the experience of senior executives with the youthful energy of the workforce. Making ourselves open to being interested and sensitive makes us feel alive and receptive to new ideas, which encourages creativity in our expression.

As a result, technological agility is now required rather than a choice. Delivering on societal and consumer expectations necessitates a collaborative learning relationship. Due to their years of experience navigating waves of change, senior executives gain a feeling of stability, and younger millennials benefit from exposure to cutting-edge technologies.

"Reverse mentorship is a crucial component of the contemporary workplace."

We examine the necessity and advantages of reverse mentoring in the modern world. Uber, Amazon, Apple, Netflix, and Swiggy are examples of modern businesses that have transformed how people engage with and consume media, music, travel, education, shopping, and food. Social media and data analytics are now crucial tools for adapting to customer preferences and thinking creatively. Although change has always been a given, technology has sped up the rate of change, placing pressure on people to act swiftly. We require knowledgeable and dependable advisers on our team, such as a parent, teacher, guide, or mentor, to help us navigate and think through changes and uncertainties.

Individuals' strengths and limitations must be balanced because practically all the necessary abilities may actually be found under one roof. In this new context, it will be crucial for organisational employees to share ideas and, at the most fundamental level, learn from one another across generational divides. This can entail talking to the team's "millennials" or Gen Y members and exchanging ideas and expertise.

The transactional analysis theory can influence relationships between various age groups. By raising self-awareness among the various age groups, the contact may be modified to be an adult-adult interaction rather than a parent-child interaction. Regardless of their age or gender, people who are self-aware can see their own distinctiveness as well as that of others and thoughtfully collaborate.

"Reverse mentorship is advantageous since it exposes the younger executive to the perspective of the more seasoned leader. The senior leader retains a sense of youth and keeps up with the times."

The way business is done has changed as a result of technology. There is now a sense of urgency, leaving little time for thought and reaction. Similar to how corporate technologies like data analytics, robots, and social media have taken centre stage thanks to recent technology developments. Over the past several decades, social interactions and tastes have also altered, making it crucial for leaders to be aware of the current situation.

Reverse mentoring can be used in a variety of ways, as described below:

- A parallel board to the executive committee might be made up of millennials who were chosen by their peers. Gen Y can have a significant impact on business decisions that determine the direction of the company.
- Reverse mentorship, where youthful workers mentor senior leadership on topics like technology, flexible work arrangements, social media savvy, and employee engagement, is becoming more and more popular in organisations.
- Reverse Mentoring is another manner in which generational gaps may be overcome. From the standpoint of organisational culture, it also highlights how learning across generations can be a powerful unifying factor and be extremely enriching for everyone involved from the standpoint of organisational culture.
- Selected millennials provide back-to-back digital tool mentoring to senior leadership, including the executive

committee and company heads. As a result, there is mutual two-way learning and sharing, and the senior leadership gains insight into the perspectives of the younger generations.

How to build a successful, long-lasting "Reverse Mentoring" partnership?

- When attempting to establish an ongoing "reverse mentoring" connection, the methods listed below may be helpful.
- The strong chemistry between enthusiastic professionals serves as the foundation of a successful mentoring relationship. It's critical to enhance one another's strengths. As a result, it's critical to pinpoint areas where a person wishes to improve, and a possible mentor partner ought to be able to do so. Here, an evaluation of one's own strengths and flaws might be useful.
- Being adaptable and open-minded are essential traits, and this goes for both the mentor and the mentee. During the encounter, it's important to keep in mind active listening and unbiased thinking.
- The connection will develop if the progress is quickly assessed, and it will also allow for any necessary course adjustments in the middle of the process. The understanding of progress can also lead to the discovery of new strategies to accomplish objectives.
- It's crucial to provide clear answers to issues up front, including What do we hope to achieve from the engagement? What talents and skills are we likely to affect? At what time and location will the meetings be held? Whether objectives are specified and accepted by

all parties.

- Communication preferences differ throughout generations. To minimise delays and misunderstandings, it will be helpful to align the preferred method of contact (whether it be by phone, email, instant messaging, or video chat). Both the mentor and the mentee must be in agreement on this matter.

Reverse mentoring, or the benefits it provides to the participating mentors, who develop essential leadership abilities while also gaining new skills and experience from their mentee, may be one of the underappreciated advantages of a successful mentoring program.

The aforementioned procedures also guarantee that reverse mentoring remains a two-way structure and that both the mentor and the mentee may use the connection to advance their own personal and professional development over time. Reverse mentoring can help firms develop and keep talent since talent engagement is a major problem in the majority of enterprises across all sectors.

How can you create a mentoring program?

One study predicts that by 2025, millennials will make up 75% of the world's workforce. As a result, millennials will make up a sizable portion of tomorrow's leaders, and they must be prepared to steer businesses in the right direction in the future. It is not surprising that firms are reconsidering methods of learning to bring up-and-coming young leaders up to speed because this is only achievable if younger employees learn the correct things and learn them effectively. One strategy is to mentor young professionals, in which senior executives give advice and direction to younger workers so they can advance to success.

The HR department and corporate executives must take ownership of mentoring initiatives. The stages that make up an excellent mentoring programme are as follows:

- Mentorship programmes can have a variety of goals, such as creating future leaders, assisting with retention, assisting with onboarding new employees, etc. Based on the company's strategy, HR and business should choose the best candidates.
- Choosing the best mentor-mentee relationships:The right mentor-mentee combo may accomplish great things. Interests and goals should be taken into consideration while choosing pairings. To assist in choosing the proper mentee, mentors should consider information about their younger workers.
- Mentors and mentees should establish clear expectations from the beginning and on an ongoing basis so that both parties know what to anticipate.
- It is critical to monitor the correct KPIs and development areas to ensure the mentorship journey is effective. But simply following the procedure is insufficient; business leaders must also think about the personality and traits of their mentees in order to choose the best assistance.

A programme for workplace mentorship is a fantastic approach for recent recruits to grow their network. It might take months for many new recruits to get to know important coworkers. A mentee's access to crucial professional relationships can be accelerated through a mentorship programme. This is especially true in settings where people work remotely.

Most mentoring programmes demand that the mentee think about their future plans or the objectives they intend to achieve as a result of the relationship. A mentorship programme provides young workers greater power over the course of their careers by urging them to think about how they may learn from the experience. According to research, employees who are mentored have a more favourable career trajectory than those who are not. This entails obtaining more pay and more promotions in addition to having a more fulfilling career.

You've come to the right spot if you work in HR, particularly in learning and development, and you want to establish or expand your company's mentorship programme. The effort involved in mentoring programmes can be significant, especially if it is done manually.

> "*A strong mentorship programme is in line with the broad organisational objectives. Senior executives are traditionally paired with less experienced ones in mentoring programmes to help them develop within the company. Increasing the number of promotions inside the company can be the aim of this kind of mentorship.*"

There are more mentorship programmes available with various goals. The following table lists several mentoring programme goals along with their associated main outcome:

- Promoting your mentorship programme should firstly centre on winning over the leadership. There will be a cascading impact on the rest of the organisation if executives support the programme and emphasise its value.

- Utilising the zeal of early adopters or well-liked mentors will spread the word about the programme and generate interest.

- Many mentoring programmes begin with a kick-off party (virtual or physical) where participants can meet other programme participants.

- Potential mentors may be researched by mentees, and they can realise that they are a part of a broader company-wide project, which will motivate them to keep the connection going.

- The most interesting and challenging aspect of the process is finding mentors and mentees. When your programme expands beyond 10 mentors and 10 mentees, manually matching mentors and mentees may turn into a logistical headache.

- Many businesses employ together's mentoring software . To effectively generate pairings using an algorithm that takes into account the responses supplied by participants in a registration form, The use of mentoring software has various benefits.

- Identify the traits of successful mentees and mentors and promote them in all participants to help build meaningful connections between mentors and mentees.

- Strong mentees and mentors should have a desire to achieve; a positive attitude; good time management skills; an open mind to new ideas; clear communication; initiative; and leadership skills or talents.

- You must concentrate on each person's objectives for what they want to gain from the mentoring relationship if you want to create a successful one.

- You might connect up the mentee with the head of sales and then foster their relationship by encouraging them to discuss how to make that transition if the mentee wants to move from marketing to sales, for example.

- If there isn't a plan or agenda to help get things going, the first meeting may be difficult. Giving the mentee questions to ask their mentor will assist in shaping the kinds of talks they have because of this.

- Make it clear why mentoring is important to the organisation and why you are promoting it. Do you offer a place for discussing professional aspirations or for practising and developing skills? Even when workers don't share an office, virtual mentoring may assist in establishing a common corporate culture by rooting the program's overarching aims in your company's principles.

- If building community is your objective, ask the mentoring pairs to consider how they can individually contribute to it and what functions they often do in their communities. Ask your couples to rebuild a process and learn from one another while doing so if the attribute is innovation and creativity.

Traditional mentoring relationships involve workers from several tenures. The more experienced mentor offers their protégé continuous counsel, including help with obstacles and professional decisions. If you are the recipient of this connection, you could benefit from it in terms of gradual advancement. However, in my experience, a mentorship that is just transactional—that is, when you are the only one learning—will eventually fade and prove to be less beneficial over time. However, transformative mentorships may assist you and your mentor, regardless of the career route you intend to take, to get ready for a fast-paced future.

Why your mentoring program needs to be required?

More than 70% of Fortune 500 firms provide some kind of mentorship to their staff members in an effort to, among other things, improve retention and performance. However, there hasn't been much concrete proof of businesses gaining such advantages. According to a recent study, mentorship programmes may actually result in positive outcomes for both individuals and their companies, but only when they are required. That's because those who most need mentoring are more likely to turn it down if it's voluntary.

I've learnt a lot about sharing knowledge, working together, and streamlining processes since being a mentor. Here are a few things to think about if you're interested in mentoring. Different fields can be represented through mentors and mentees. Mentorship may take place between coworkers in the same discipline or across them. I have served as a mentor to nurses, instructional designers, and IT professionals. Even when I was mentoring someone from a different field of expertise, I continued to learn about communication, process improvement, and general problem-solving techniques. I now promote nursing staff members' engaging in mentoring relationships with non-nursing coworkers.

> *"It's not necessary for a mentor to have more experience than their mentee."*

The ideal way to think of a mentor is as an advisor—someone who offers a unique viewpoint and specific professional expertise. Having said that, they cannot, and shouldn't, decide for you in the end. They are unable to perform the tasks that you both agree are required. Be ready to choose the best possible option for yourself and to put in the additional effort, such as training or studying for a certification exam.

Employees are becoming concerned. People's perspectives on their connection to work have fundamentally changed as a result of the epidemic. People are basically voting with their feet as they reevaluate the meaning of work by connecting it to their bigger purpose in terms of what they want out of life. The widespread challenges with employee engagement and retention that mentoring may address are finally being recognised by businesses. To further assist in painting the image, I've highlighted other instances of mentorship facts and statistics below.

- According to the PwC reasearch, at least 65% of people were looking for a new job in 2023. Until 2022, that pattern is most likely to persist. Leaders who sponsor or coach others are twice as likely to be aware of their subordinates' concerns.
- According to the Gallup reasearch, employee turnover costs US businesses nearly $1 trillion per year because it can cost up to twice as much to hire a new employee. 66% percent of employees who sponsor, coach, or mentor others are satisfied with their ability to complete difficult projects.
- According to a CNBC report, mentored employees are significantly less likely to consider leaving their jobs (individual contributor, manager, senior manager, and vice president, to name a few). 90% of employees who have a mentor are satisfied with their jobs.
- According to a Linkedin survey report, if their business provided additional possibilities for learning and

professional growth, 94% of employees would remain longer.

- According to a DDI report, the three main factors that women should consider when deciding whether to become mentors are their relationship with the mentee (54%), subject matter knowledge (54%), and time commitment (75%). The majority of other criteria, such as the mentee's age (4%) and gender (2%), tend not to matter.
- According to the MentorcliQ research data, participating in mentorship programmes increases employee retention by 50% compared to non-participants, and 93% of mentees think their mentoring relationship was beneficial.
- According to University of Olivet Nazarene, confirmed that those who reported having a mentor, 81% indicated that their mentor was employed by the same company, and 61% said that their mentor was employed by the same institution. According to 41% of respondents, formal goals are part of their mentoring relationship.

As a result, businesses are considering mentoring as a means of achieving their talent objectives. Additionally, recent polls, research, and publications seem to support that. Linkedin survey report says that greater percentage of employees said they would stay longer if their business provided more possibilities for learning and professional advancement. 93% of mentees think their mentoring relationship was beneficial, and employees who participate in mentoring programmes have a retention rate that is 50% higher than those who do not.

"Businesses that invest in their employees keep their top talent."

- According to the Coqual report, those who volunteer to be a sponsor, mentor, or coach are more likely to benefit from their own skill development.The majority (57%) increase their skill sets, compared to 40% of non-sponsors; 41% are more likely to take on tasks they dislike; 43% increase their understanding of their customer base; and 30% increase their understanding of potential new customers or market segments, compared to 26% of non-sponsors.

- Today's workforce prefers companies that embrace inclusion, equity, and diversity. According to a CNBC report, 80% of workers want to work for organisations that place a high priority on DEI. And while research on the advantages of mentoring and its favourable effects on women in the workplace has grown significantly over the past several years, I have found that there is a dearth of information on how mentoring benefits workers who identify as BIPOC or LGBTQ+. More studies and data will be required to show the advantages and gaps in mentoring for many employees among historically underrepresented groups as DEI becomes more significant to corporate culture.

- According to the DDI report, if their company has a structured mentoring programme, women are 10% more likely to accept a request to be a mentor. 70% of women who mentor other women, they do so out of a desire to help other women. Only 54% of women say they have ever been asked to serve as a professional mentor.

- According to the MentorcliQ research data, 38% of employees, the most preferred DEI mentoring programme format is traditional 1-to-1 mentoring. The next closest group, 31%, has a strong preference for 1:1 reverse mentorship. 80% of workers, DEI mentoring programmes' main motivators are inclusion, sponsorship, allyship, involvement, and skill-building.
- The job market is rapidly altering in appearance. Millennials (aged 25–44 in 2025) will make up 42.5% of the workforce, according to Alight (previously NGA Human Resources), while Gen Z will make up 28.2%. (aged 16 to 24). The upcoming decade will be crucial for Millennials' future job movements in particular. As a result, Millennials (and Gen Z) are beginning to consider issues like skill development, job growth, and quality of life more carefully.
- According to Deloitte report 49% of Millennials plan to quit their jobs within the next two years. Millennials are more inclined to leave their jobs since there are fewer prospects for professional growth (35%), as well as for learning and development (28%). Millennials who stay at their company for five or more years have a mentor in 68% of cases, compared to 32% of those who don't.
- According to the Forbes research data, learning is very important to Gen Z, with 76% of them seeing it as essential to their professional development.
- According to the CNBC data, when compared to individuals who don't have mentors, millennial and generation z workers who have mentors are 21% to 23% more likely to say they are content with their present position.
- According to Randstad report, participating employees were 49% less likely to leave, and the cost savings from

hiring and training were about $3,000 per person each year.

- According to the SHRM research data, says when they sense their boss cares about them, 73% of Gen Z are inspired to do better.

A little shout-out You may do so right now for free if you're an HR professional or a people leader wanting to launch a mentorship programme quickly. You may access the whole mentorship platform of together by completing a short form. You may swiftly send out registration invitations to your staff members, and we'll match them up depending on what's important to each of them. If you think this would be something you'd be interested in trying, find out more about how we make employee connection simple.

Both the mentee and the mentor stand to gain a variety of advantages from a mentoring arrangement. In fact, most HR professionals polled for our State of Mentorship and Coaching Report saw coaching and mentoring as having advantages for mentees. Being mentored by a more seasoned and mature individual has several advantages. A mentor can hasten your learning and growth rather than relying just on your own experience.

> *"Organisations that offer professional help in the workplace should anticipate attracting talent and seeing higher retention rates with those they do."*

More effectively than work training, providing career mentors to less experienced employees fosters their skill development and social connections with the company. Employees like to develop more holistically through cultivating connections with mentors rather than acquiring new skills and being judged on them.

- According to Gallup, which has been researching employee engagement since 2000, more than 50% of U.S. workers are disengaged with their jobs. The achievement of organisational objectives and success depend on employee involvement. They are the workers that propel the company ahead and inspire others to follow suit.

Disengagement has an antidote in mentoring. Encourage workers to have frequent one-on-one meetings with a mentor who can offer them feedback and serve as a sounding board for them to discuss their objectives and obstacles they must face in order to achieve them in order to re-engage them.

Fostering an inclusive and diverse workplace diversity and inclusion are essential to a company's development, effectiveness, and strength. According to a number of studies, diverse workforces are linked to better incomes. The research showed that companies with senior management roles for women had a 10% boost in cash flow returns on investment.

- According to a McKinsey study, businesses with greater ethnic and ethical diversity had a 35% higher chance of experiencing increased revenue. Having a workplace mentorship programme is crucial if your company wants to foster a more diverse and inclusive workplace. Employees may communicate, benefit from one another's knowledge, and develop through mentoring.

- According to research by Google, new recruits who were matched with a mentor reached full effectiveness 25% faster than their colleagues who weren't assigned a suitable mentor.

Career advancement and mentoring go hand in hand. With so many professionals seeking out mentoring connections to grow in their professions, mentoring is now regarded as one of the top tactics for career development and progression. Mentorship has also been shown to be quite helpful in assisting and directing those who are trying to change careers. It's advantageous for your career whether you're a mentor or a mentee.

> *"In the face of these difficulties, mentoring can support us in remaining strong and connected. It may be necessary for various employers to create different distinctions between their personal and professional lives, and the mentor and mentee will finally decide on the particular arrangement."*

Successful mentoring relationships are the foundation of effective workplace mentoring initiatives. More significantly, mentoring with a solid connection at its foundation will benefit participants and the organisation the most. It is crucial to report on your mentoring programme because you want to show stakeholders, such as leadership or other workers, who are debating whether a mentoring connection is worthwhile, the outcomes of the relationships you helped foster.

In conclusion, employees are becoming concerned. People's perspectives on their connection to work have fundamentally changed as a result of the epidemic. People are basically voting with their feet as they reevaluate the meaning of work by connecting it to their bigger purpose in terms of what they want out of life. The widespread challenges with employee engagement and retention that mentoring may address are finally being recognised by businesses.

"Mentorship may provide stability in a period of great upheaval, instability in the workplace, and suffocating loneliness. Successful mentoring involves considerably more active listening than one-way advice giving, and when done from a point of reciprocity, mentors may reap significant rewards."

- Dr. Amit Das

References

- *The Soul of a Team: A Modern-Day Fable for Winning Teamwork Hardcover – January 22, 2019 by Tony Dungy (Author), Nathan Whitaker.*
- *The HEART of Laser-Focused Coaching: A Revolutionary Approach to Masterful Coaching Paperback – September 25, 2019 by Marion Franklin (Author).*
- *Techniques for Coaching and Mentoring 1st Edition by David Megginson (Author), David Clutterbuck (Author) 2019.*
- *10 Steps to Successful Mentoring (10 Steps Series) Paperback – June 25, 2019 by Wendy Axelrod (Author).*
- *Backstage Leadership: The Invisible Work of Highly Effective Leaders 1st ed. 2020 Edition by Charles Galunic (Author).*
- *Athena Rising: How and Why Men Should Mentor Women Hardcover – September 20, 2016 by W. Brad Johnson (Author), David Smith (Author).*
- *The Everything Coaching and Mentoring Book: How to increase productivity, foster talent, and encourage success Paperback – January 1, 2008 by Nicholas Nigro (Author).*
- *Coaching and Mentoring in the Asia Pacific (Routledge EMCC Masters in Coaching and Mentoring) 1st Edition by Anna Blackman (Editor), Derrick Kon (Editor), David Clutterbuck (Editor).*
- *Coaching and Mentoring: Theory and Practice Third Edition by Robert Garvey (Author), Paul Stokes (Author), David Megginson (Author).*
- *Coaching and Mentoring for Work-Life Balance (Routledge EMCC Masters in Coaching and Mentoring)*

1st Edition by Julie Haddock-Millar (Author), Eliot Tom (Author).

- *Peer Supervision in Coaching and Mentoring: A Versatile Guide for Reflective Practice 1st Edition by Tammy Turner (Author), Michelle Lucas (Author), Carol Whitaker (Author).*
- *Coaching, Mentoring and Managing: Breakthrough Strategies to Solve Performance Problems and Build Winning Teams Paperback – January 1, 1996 by William & Sam Bartlett & Joe Gilliam & Kit Grant & Jack MacKey & Bob Hendricks (Author).*
- *Coaching and Mentoring for Academic Development (Surviving and Thriving in Academia) by Kay Guccione (Author), Steve Hutchinson (Author).*
- *Developing Mentoring and Coaching Relationships in Early Care and Education: A Reflective Approach (Practical Resources in ECE) 1st Edition by Marilyn Chu (Author).*
- *The Art of Listening in Coaching and Mentoring (Routledge EMCC Masters in Coaching and Mentoring) 1st Edition by Stephen Burt (Author).*
- *Coaching and Mentoring Research: A Practical Guide 1st Edition by Lindsay G. Oades (Author), Christine Leanne Siokou (Author), Gavin R. Slemp (Author).*
- *Coaching and Mentoring Skills (NetEffect Series) 1st Edition by Andrew J. DuBrin (Author).*
- *Leadership Coaching, Mentoring, Counselling or Supervision? One Way Is Not Enough Hardcover – September 1, 2020 by Karene Biggs Eileen Piggot-Irvine (Author).*
- *The Mentoring, Coaching, and Leadership Development Workbook (Marketplace Edition): A Workbook for Leaders Who Want to Empower Others Paperback – April 13, 2021 by Dr. Paul G. Leavenworth (Author).*

- *How To Be A Good Leader: A Step-By-Step Approach To Coaching, Mentoring, And Developing Others: How To Coach Employees For Improved Performance Paperback – August 9, 2021 by Princess Dort (Author).*
- *The Mentor That Matters: Stories of Transformational Teachers, Role Models and Heroes, Volume 1 Paperback – November 21, 2016 by Suzanne Fox (Author, Editor), Laura Steward Atchison (Author).*
- *The Leader's Guide to Coaching and Mentoring: How to Use Soft Skills to Get Hard Results Paperback – October 19, 2015 by Fiona Elsa Dent (Author), Mike Brent (Author).*
- *The Mentoring Manual: Your Step by Step Guide to Being a Better Mentor Paperback – November 1, 2014 by Julie Starr (Author).*

About The Author

Dr. Amit Das, is a renowned executive advisor, consultant, educationist, author, speaker, counsellor, and coach whose 25+ years of business experience provides high-impact, practical solutions that support his clients' leadership development and organisational transformations. He worked for three great fortune 500 MNCs and left rich leagacy of organising transformational learning workshops. He has transformed more than 5000+ working executives through his path breaking soft skills training workshops. Dr. Amit Das is recognised as an innovative, principled thought leader who combines intellectual rigor and discipline with an ability to translate theory into practice. His operational skills are coupled with a strategic ability to analyse, develop, and implement successful strategies for profitability, growth, and sustainability.

Dr. Amit Das has a successful track record in aligning learning and training solutions to key business strategy with a strong focus on flawless execution excellence to facilitate individual, business divisional, and organisational performance. He keeps relentless focus on measuring training impact and ROI, people capability building graphs, training process governance, performance coaching, and strategic thinking. These have been some of his key individual success traits. His core capabilities include performance coaching, designing training and development frameworks, psychometric assessment and analysis, competency framework development and assessments, content design and facilitation of soft skills and leadership programmes, Learning Management Systems, Learning Impact Measurement, Talent Analysis, and Performance Coaching and Counselling.

ABOUT THE AUTHOR

Dr. Amit Das has authored multiple management and self-development books, like Create Your Leadership Edge, Building Organisational Capability, Ethical Road Map, Attomic Attention, BYPB, Implementor, ALOUD, Redefining Talent Management, Defining Your Success Factors, Lead or Plead, Make The Most Of Your Life, Better Half or Bitter Half, Organisational Transformation Through Learning, The Transformative Mind & Soul are few of them.

He has a Ph.D. and a Fellowship in strategic learning, along with his first class degrees in Human Resource Management, Marketing Management, International Business, and Corporate Laws from the top business schools in India. He is a certified Psychometric analyst, HR Metrics, OD Interventionist, Human Psychologist, Lifecoach, Leadership Developer, Black Belt (LSS), Strategic Thinker, Talent Analyst, certified professional trainer from the U.K. and certified behavioral coach from the U.S.A.

Dr. Amit Das likes googling, reading books, writing articles & books, cooking, listening to old melodies, and counselling people to unleash their true potential to build a strong nation. He is married and blessed with a son. He would love to hear about your experience after reading his books. You can email him and share your thoughts, or you can use his services for life coaching, positive behavioural counseling, educational support, and mentoring for young, promising students pursuing their B.B.A. and M.B.A. degrees.

www.ingramcontent.com/pod-product-compliance
Lightning Source LLC
Chambersburg PA
CBHW021212130726
47988CB00002B/617